The Economic and Social Impact of Investments in Public Transit

The Economic and Social Impact of Investments in Public Transit

Nancy W. Sheldon
Robert Brandwein

Harbridge House, Inc.

with the assistance of
Hiroko Sakai and
Frank Remley

Lexington Books
D.C. Heath and Company
Lexington, Massachusetts
Toronto   London

HE
4461
.S5

Library of Congress Cataloging in Publication Data

Sheldon, Nancy W.
   The economic and social impact of investments in public transit.

   1. Local transit—United States—Finance. 2. Cost effectiveness. I. Brand-
wein, Robert, joint author. II. Title.
HE4461.S5   388.4'042   73-10074
ISBN 0-669-90837-1

Published simultaneously in Canada.

Printed in the United States of America.

International Standard Book Number: 0-669-90837-1

Library of Congress Catalog Card Number: 73-10074

Contents

List of Figures

List of Tables

Acknowledgments

This study was conducted by the professional staff of Harbridge House, Inc., for the United States Department of Transportation (DOT) under Contract No. DOT-OS-20182. Those staff members who made significant research, written, and review contributions were Hiroko Sakai and Frank Remley. Shirley Landon provided valuable research assistance. Sybil Carey performed able and tireless editorial assistance in both the preparation of this book and the original study for the U.S. Department of Transportation.

Charles D. Baker, President of Harbridge House, Inc., and formerly Assistant Secretary of Transportation for Policy and International Affairs, U.S. Department of Transportation, was a major contributor to this study in the conceptualization of the approach and a critical review of our effort as well as in introducing a policy realism to our findings.

A multitude of government agencies and private organizations gave us access to documents and data. However, we wish to make particular note of the outstanding assistance we received from the Library staff at the U.S. Department of Transportation. They were always courteous, pleasant, and professionally helpful, and we are grateful to them.

Special thanks are also due to Katharine Houghton for her outstanding secretarial and administrative assistance.

Nancy W. Sheldon

Robert Brandwein

Introduction

Today's government decisionmakers are faced with a policy question vis-à-vis urban transportation; that is, should urban transportation policy be directed toward making provision solely or very heavily for the highway/auto mode, or should increasing provisions be made for developing, expanding, and/or improving one or more of the public transit modes?

It is clear that bus, rapid rail, and commuter transit will not eliminate private automobile travel within metropolitan areas. It is also clear, however, that public transit—at least in certain specific situations—is a desirable alternative to the auto mode as a result of favorable social and economic impacts which a transit system can generate.

Purpose of the Study

The purpose of this study is to provide data and guidelines on public transit, in order to assist government decisionmakers faced with the responsibility of designing policies on the allocation of capital investments for urban transportation. Implicit within this statement of purpose is the concept that the findings of the study are directed toward providing insight into the logic or non-logic of using portions of federal highway excise taxes to support such capital investments in bus, rapid rail, and commuter transit systems.

Much has been written, and more has been said, concerning the benefits of public transit to society. Similarly, volumes have been generated suggesting that such benefits are transitory at best and nonexistent at worst. On conducting this study, we have reviewed the record, assessed the evidence, and evaluated the potential social and economic impacts of increased governmental focus on public transit. Toward this end, we have reviewed and analyzed an enormous number of investigations and studies published by consultants and the members of the academic community, statements and statistical information issued by leaders in the transit industry, pertinent journal and news articles, relevant studies prepared by city planners and urban-design architects, and progress reports and other documents on capital grant programs submitted to the U.S. Department of Transportation (DOT).

Methodology

The methodology used during the course of this study began with an examination and evaluation of the aforementioned documents for evidence and examples of social and economic impact which have resulted or are projected to result from capital investments in public transit systems. The findings were then ordered in terms applicable to goal-achievement analysis. The reasons for using goal-achievement analysis and a description of this particular methodology are the subject of the paragraphs which follow.

Regardless of whether economic, social, cultural, or educational in nature, or who the beneficiaries are, the impacts of any public transportation program have several dimensions to consider. Consequently, decisions concerning a choice of alternative transportation investments require some systematic means of contrasting all the alternatives in terms of potential benefits relative to costs incurred.

Cost-benefit analysis has been frequently employed to assist decisionmakers faced with the task of measuring the effects of various types of public investments projects (that is, water resource developments, highway construction, and so forth). However, this approach, as traditionally applied, suffers from a serious shortcoming in that it primarily relies on the criterion of economic efficiency for judging the acceptability of a program or for selecting one from among several different proposals competing for the same investment resources. Consequently, the resulting decision frequently contains a bias in favor of choosing projects with the highest level of monetary performance. Intangible benefits which can be pervasive and highly significant are generally not included due to the problems involved in applying monetary measurements to intangibles.

Specifically, with regard to transportation program decisions, the traditional cost-benefit analysis would be a perfectly adequate tool if the financial viability of a proposed program, or programs, was the primary concern. However, decisions which also encompass a wide array of transportation-related socioeconomic consequences often prove to be superior both from the standpoint of social equality and optimum allocation of public funds. Goal-achievement analysis is an expanded form of traditional cost-benefit analysis which provides decisionmakers with a tool for evaluating tangible and nontangible impacts related to a specific project.[1]

For evaluating the social and economic value of a particular transportation program or for contrasting alternative model choices, goal-achievement analysis requires that several steps are followed:

1. Identify all community goals to be achieved through transportation investments (for example, improve the economic welfare of urban residents).
2. Translate the goals into specific achievable objectives (for example, increase employment opportunities). This permits the level of achievement projected to be realized through a particular program to be evaluated directly in terms of the costs and benefits (or dis-benefits) related to each of the specified objectives (for example, a net increase in jobs created may be converted to wages earned).
3. Weight each goal, thus creating a hierarchy of goals which is politically acceptable and realistic in terms of priority and urgency.

4. Determine the benefits, dis-benefits, and costs resulting from a program's impact on an objective.
   a. A quantitatively defended objective can have its benefits, dis-benefits, and costs measured in either monetary or nonmonetary units. The latter can be sometimes converted to monetary values by making use of empirical information. For example, air pollution levels can be expressed by specific measurable units, such as the amount of pollutants per unit volume of air. The level then can be converted into a monetary value based on social costs and benefits; for example, the increase or decrease in the amount of money involved in installing antipollution devices, the potential medical expenditures for those who suffer ailments caused by breathing poor quality air, costs of laundry bills, painting and washing of the exterior of buildings and houses, and so forth.
   b. Many of the intangible types of objectives may not be amenable to quantitative measurement of the level of consequences. These consequences should then be expressed in as explicit terms as possible, in order to indicate the extent to which the objective is or is not achieved. For example, aesthetic impact considerations related to transportation planning may have to be stated in terms of a descriptive ranking classification, (such as high degree of impact, moderate degree of impact, and so forth).
5. The minimum level of benefits or maximum allowable level of costs or dis-benefits pertaining to each objective must be established.
6. Due to the fact that benefits, dis-benefits, and costs from taking a specific course of action accrue at different time periods, the measurements of consequences must be converted to their value or cost equivalents at a common point in time (for example, discounting).
7. When the goal-achievement evaluation information is assembled into a format (see Table I-1), the benefits, dis-benefits, and costs expressed as common units are totaled. The totals can then be used either for watching the progress of a particular project over time or for comparing the levels of achievement for two or more projects over time.

In this study we have not performed a complete goal achievement analysis. However, starting with generally agreed upon broad urban goals (limited to those deemed feasible within a current time framework and to those for which achievement levels could be related to specific urban transportation objectives) related urban transportation objectives were identified.[2] Table I-2 lists the set of broad urban goals, while Figure I-1 graphically illustrates the primary links between these goals and the objectives (as defined in Part I) in terms of measuring achievement levels. Then:

1. The urban transportation objectives were examined and evaluated with respect to impacts on them by bus, rapid rail, and commuter transit. The

Table I-1
Illustrative Goal Achievement Evaluation Chart

Goal Description (in terms of transportation-related objectives) Relative Value Assigned	Time-savings 2			Air Pollution Abatement 3			Employment 1		
Incidence Groups/Localities — Relative Value Assigned	Benefits	Dis-benefits	Costs	Benefits	Dis-benefits	Costs	Benefits	Dis-benefits	Costs
Ghetto Area A — 3									
Ghetto Area B — 2									
Central Business District — 3									
Suburban Communities — 2									
Total									

Table I-2
Broad Urban Goals*

- Revitalize the economic base of our inner-city areas. Slow down and reverse the trends of deterioration and mass exodus from urban centers.
- Increase social welfare. Improve the number and quality of social amenities available to inner-city residents. Improve the delivery of services.
- Increase freedom of choice and ability to participate in urban opportunities for all members of the urban population.
- Improve the quality of the urban environment. Produce a more healthy environment, together with more efficient and aesthetic utilization of urban space.
- Achieve more equitable income distribution.

*Listing is not by order of importance or by level of priority.

impacts were expressed in terms of economic efficiency and equity (see Introduction to Part I).

2. Individual programs, by geographic area, were analyzed for evidence of specific impact on the transportation objectives. Additional objectives were also developed and modifications fed back into the original list of objectives.

3. From the findings of the study, several policy guidelines were developed.

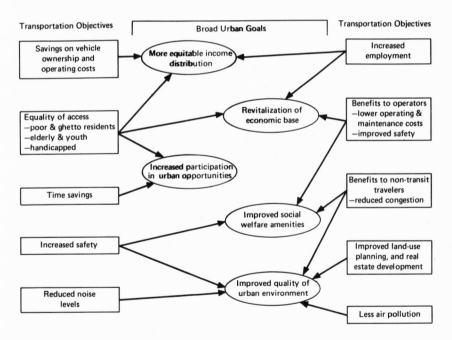

Figure I-1. Broad Urban Goals and Transportation Objectives: Flow Chart of Primary Linkages.

As can be seen in reviewing the steps undertaken during the study, we did not apply weight to the goals, and therefore did not perform a complete goal achievement analysis because the ranking process requires the participation of persons actively involved in setting and defining public policy goals. The assignment of weighting factors by persons in non-policy-making positions (for example, economists) may result in a distortion or bias of the analysis.

Organization of the Report

In Part I, each objective is discussed in detail. Part II presents the results of our case findings for several specific transit systems. Finally, our findings are summarized and the conclusions to the study in the form of policy guidelines are presented in Part III.

Part I
Evaluation of the Impacts of Public Transit on the Objectives of Public Transportation

Introduction

As described in the Introduction to this volume, broad urban goals are identified and related to a set of urban transportation objectives designed to help achieve these goals. In Part I, the role of public transit in meeting these objectives is examined. The urban transportation objectives have been organized into three categories, according to the type of impacted group: users, operators, and the community or general public.

Initially, in analyzing whether or not public transit makes a contribution to meeting the various urban transportation objectives, the objectives were evaluated in terms of the concepts of economic efficiency and equity.[1] There are, however, as one observer has indicated,[2] four basic limitations in relying solely on these economic concepts for evaluating the impact of transit on the urban transportation objectives:

1. Cost differences among alternative plans are usually minimal, particularly in view of the assumptions on which future travel patterns are forecast.
2. Traditionally, consideration has not been given to including measurable (or nonmeasurable) community costs in the analyses. Moreover, methods for giving adequate consideration to social and environmental factors should be improved.
3. There is a tendency to minimize the magnitude of public transport investment. In some cases this produces operationally unworkable systems. In other cases, the tendency to freeze development goals and plans before the transport system is considered may also add to capital and operating costs.
4. The smaller scale of center-city improvements and their land-use impacts makes it difficult to systematically detect differences among alternatives.

Moreover, in the past, economic efficiency and equity have been widely used as the sole criteria for evaluating the benefits and costs of various proposed highway projects. As a result, certain biases have unintentionally become incorporated into the evaluations. These biases have created real difficulties whenever attempts have been made to evaluate or compare public transit within the same limited framework. As illustrated in the following cases, some of the biases which have appeared from the evaluation of highway projects in terms of efficiency and equity have taken the form of accounting deficiencies.[3]

1. *Valuation of land required for transportation system.* Under accounting procedures which strictly emphasize cash flow, the varying cost of land to the

government highway sponsor is nil, since he pays no taxes on it. However, in truth, land taken for publicly-owned transportation incurs an opportunity cost in terms of real estate taxes that are lost. If these costs are not considered in the feasibility analyses of transportation plans, an unwarranted bias in favor of land-intensive modes—namely highways—would exist.

Likewise, planners often use only the acquisition cost of land for developing a transportation feasibility analysis, setting aside present and future social costs of acquiring that land from a limited supply. For instance, urban transportation systems sometimes require land that could otherwise be used for housing, retail, or industrial facilities by private owners. As a result, the value of that land, in terms of lost income or social costs, may be much greater than the price paid for it. Therefore, using acquisition price alone also biases the planning process in favor of highways.

Finally, to the extent that urban transportation systems consume valuable urban land, making it increasingly expensive for new companies to expand productive capacity economically, the social cost of acquiring urban land for transportation should include a factor for the disruption of the competitive markets and greater economies of scale. It stands to reason, then, that if one industry or company has dominated the economic resources of an area, making it difficult and expensive for new industries, whose goods might be closely substitutable, to enter the scene, the price of goods would be higher than they would otherwise be. In addition, it tends to promote a locally imperfect market structure, insofar as prices and output are not optimum; and this results in a definite social cost, which, if not attached somehow to the acquisition price of land, would lead to another bias in favor of highways.

2. *Inadequate accounting of nonmarket costs which are attributable to highway expansion.* Highway planners have a tendency not to estimate the monetary cost of such social burdens as air pollution, increased noise levels, dislocation of long-term residents and the associated breakdown of local social institutions, and the sometimes bizarre assortment of roadside development and concomitant visual pollution that often accompanies highway expansions. It is admittedly difficult to place reliable economic values on these social burdens, but to assume they have zero value is an infinitely more erroneous bias in favor of highways.

3. *Improper accounting of the long-term effects of highway extensions.* While highway planners are quick to derive estimates for savings in time and efficiency associated with new highways, they often fail to be completely cognizant of these savings over the long run. It has been shcwn that new highways, because of their traffic inducement qualities, will often be much slower and more congested several years later than was ever considered initially. This is in part due to a congestion-shifting effect in which secondary road users spill onto the freeways in greater numbers than anticipated, over and above the new highway users from new developments and new employment induced by

the highway. Therefore, this overstatement of the value of time savings and efficiency is also a planning bias in favor of highway expansion.

In addition, during the process of preparing the review and analysis which follow, it became evident that the urban transportation objectives as set forth in the Introduction to this volume both complement and serve as substitutes for purely economic indicators in that, when implemented, they make a resource allocation more efficient and, when applicable, more equitable. For example, objectives such as equality of access, increased employment, improved environmental impact, and savings on vehicle ownership and operating costs tend toward "equity" (a positive relationship). In contrast, some aspects of the objective related to better land use planning and real estate development, while allocating resources "efficiently," may not distribute income in a manner deemed equitable to society (a negative relationship).

It should be kept in mind that, in terms of efficiency and equity, the automobile driver who does not use public transit can, nevertheless, benefit from investments in public transit. For example, increased use of public transit which diverts people from automobile travel will have a strong impact on motorists in that every 50 persons diverted to public transit represent a reduction of approximately 30 automobiles in the traffic stream, with a consequent easing of downtown traffic and parking congestion.

Finally, the auto driver as a member of the community or general public directly receives the positive impacts deriving from public transit as discussed in this Part, such as reduction of air pollution, improved economic vitality of the city, lower accident levels, and so forth.

For the above reasons, our discussion in Part I necessarily goes beyond the economic questions and into areas of social benefits, which although perhaps not quantifiable are necessary inputs for the decisionmaker. The remainder of this Part evaluates the effects of public transit on each objective in as much detail as is currently available in the literature.

1 User Benefits

Equality of Access

General

Of all the benefits which may develop from public transit, the most often cited is the ability of transit systems to provide to all persons mobility and equality of access to the employment, cultural, health, and educational opportunities of urban areas. However, President Nixon, in his message to the Congress on March 18, 1971, summarized the nation's transit situation as follows:

Approximately 95 percent of all travel in urbanized areas is by automobile; yet about 25 percent of our people—especially the old, the young, the poor, and the handicapped—do not drive a car. They have been poorly served by our transportation strategy.[1]

The quotation below, taken from a report by the consulting group of Parsons, Brinckerhoff, Tudor, Bechtel, Sverdrup & Parcel, exemplifies most writing which is concerned with meeting the needs of captive riders through the supply of transit.[2]

It is sometimes difficult to remember, when faced by the profusion of cars on American streets, that approximately half of any urban population cannot avail itself of this convenience. The young, the old, the handicapped, those that refuse to drive, and those who cannot afford a car are all in a very disadvantageous position in a modern metropolis without public transportation. Children and teenagers must be transported by others to cultural and recreational facilities; the elderly, and mothers with small children, cannot reach medical centers; those who are physically infirm cannot even reach shops. These people very often live in an environment that ignores their needs completely and deprives them of many of the cultural, recreational, business, and medical services and opportunities that society should provide.

The question of basic mobility is particularly significant today when all major activities are at concentrated and therefore distant points from residences, and when the entire metropolitan scale has gone beyond the walking dimension. In large regions, a bus system alone (which may very well be inferior) cannot satisfy access needs, since some of the more important special activities will probably be a discouragingly long travel time away. A superior rapid transit system can help to remedy this situation, and consequently provide many other specific benefits. These range from reduced dormitory requirements at local colleges, since students can utilize other accommodations, to better patronage at sporting events.

5

In many old cities, however, the above-mentioned considerations pale into insignificance when compared to the plight of low-income residents. More important, that is, than lack of access to services is lack of access to jobs, especially for unskilled, semi-skilled, and blue-collar workers.

Not too many decades ago, industrial and service workers who lived in the central city were able to reach their jobs easily, since they too were located in the built-up area, and were reasonably dispersed there. Lately, however, many factories have moved to suburbs to escape city problems, and many industries have been eliminated entirely or have undergone internal modifications resulting in changed labor demands. At the same time, the less-skilled workers, whose choices in employment are most restricted, have congregated into the inner city ghettos.

The result is a serious geographic mismatch of work places and residences for those people who are least capable economically of overcoming distances. These underemployed workers are forced into an ever-deepening economic depression. Their movement demands are most legitimate, and their consumption of welfare funds could be lessened considerably if jobs were available and accessible. The social consequences are potentially dangerous unless some answers are found.

One of the best currently available solutions to this problem is rapid transit.[3]

There are, nevertheless, two types of opinion which stand in opposition to those who acclaim the benefits of this aspect of public transportation. First, there is the argument that more and more costly rapid transit systems are serving only the captive riders, and thus not efficiently using public funds in view of the relatively small size of this market.[4] Second, but related to the prior argument, is the case that captive riders would be more efficiently served by personal rather than mass transit.[5]

In conjunction with the first point, it has been estimated that the so-called captive rider minority exceeds 52 million people, or about 26 percent of the population.[6] There is also an important characteristic—worthy of careful consideration—in the concentration of those persons and the opportunities to which they desire access. For example, in a recent article in *Civil Engineering*, Martin Wohl presented the following statistical facts:

- Of the metropolitan-area workers belonging to households without an automobile, 80 percent live within central cities.
- More than 60 percent of the urban poor, those that can least afford private transportation, live within the central cities.
- Though suburbs are more populous than central cities, about 55 percent of those 65 and older, another group that can least afford private transportation, reside in central cities.
- Most *downtown workers* live not in the suburbs but in the central cities. For U.S. cities with a population of one million or more, about 75 percent of downtown workers live within the central city. These percentages range from a low of 53 for Boston, to about 90 for New York City.
- Though the largest single concentration of urban jobs is in the downtown area, by far most jobs are in the suburbs. New York and Philadelphia have the highest percentages of jobs in the downtown area, about 28 and 29 percent. On the low end, Chicago has only 14 percent of its urban jobs downtown. In

all these cities, the percent of urban jobs within downtown areas is declining rapidly, and absolute downtown employment levels are falling in most cities.
● Thus the commuter problem is basically *not a suburban* commuter problem. Instead, the focus of mass transit should be on the central city, where workers are concentrated, where densities are high enough to make mass transit feasible.[7]

The second issue raised—that of personal versus mass transit—is not to be totally discounted. There are, however, questions related to the present state of technology and management of personal transit systems which have yet to be answered, such as: "What backup procedures are feasible? Are there any unsuspected operational problems? Who will use the system? What will they pay for the service? Why are they using it?"[8] It is to such an end that the UMTA "dial-a-bus" demonstration project is dedicated.

In addition, application of the Dial-A-Ride concept to meet the transportation needs of poor or old persons involves the basic requirement of generating awareness of the service and the mechanics of its operation. This requirement is essential since the system requires a summoning role on the part of the captive riders who must phone for service. Studies have shown that uneducated persons—who may constitute a greater proportion among the poor than among the higher income patrons—remain unwilling to clarify a matter which confuses them by actively seeking information. While this continued experimentation will indeed produce interesting concepts and ideas, we must respond now to the needs of the captive rider and do so in terms of conventional systems.

The Poor and Ghetto Residents

One of the most striking statements to appear in recent years in support of providing adequate transit to serve lower income persons has come out of the McCone Commission investigation. The commission found that

... An important factor in the hostility underlying the Watts riot was the sense of isolation due to the inadequate transportation system right spank in the middle of the most motorized city in the United States. The isolation was pervasive, extending even to services intended to benefit the inhabitants of the area; it required a bus ride of up to two hours to reach the County General Hospital, or an hour and forty-five minutes to get to the Youth Employment Training Center.[9]

The nature of the transportation needs of the poor may be grasped, above all, in terms of the problem posed by unavailability of a private automobile. In 1964, of the 9.9 million households across the nation with incomes under $3,000, 46 percent had no car.[10] By 1970 there had been little improvement in the statistics. At that time it was estimated that four out of every ten families with average annual income levels under $4,000 did not own automobiles.[11] As for the metropolitan poor, an even greater proportion of families are without an automobile. For example, in densely populated eastern Massachusetts, 65 percent of all families earning less than $4,000 a year were autoless in 1963.[12] Similarly, a study of Boston's black ghetto found 68 percent of households to be without an automobile.[13] In Los Angeles, the most motorized city in the United States, it was estimated that in 1960, 2.3 million persons—or more than 68 percent of the population—lacked regular access to automobile transportation. This category of people includes heads of households without an automobile, housewives of families with no car or one car, and teenagers as well as preteens (10 to 15 years of age—the age group which starts requiring individual mobility) for whom ready access to means of travel is severely limited.

Further compounding this problem is the fact that many of the automobiles owned by the poor are not in reliable condition. In fact, a study of automobile conditions in Watts indicated that 20 percent are not in a condition for safe driving on expressways, and 40 percent are uninsured.[14] Despite these facts, poor people's dependence on the automobile for mobility—in many instances in the form of car-pooling, borrowing, or even hitchhiking arrangements—is observed to be very high, similar to persons of higher income groups who depend on their own automobiles. In eastern Massachusetts, it was found that in 1968 63 percent of all work trips by poor household members were made as passengers in someone else's car.[15] Because dependence on someone else—the owner-driver—severely curtails flexibility in terms of scheduling trips which might be required in any work situation, lack of ready access to any direction or distance other than one for which a person has car-pooling arrangements makes it virtually impossible for him to explore new and better job opportunities. Riding with someone else is particularly limiting in terms of making nonwork trips at odd times or to out-of-the-way locations.

Significantly, due to the strong correlation between income and car ownership, one of the most pervasive findings of various transit feasibility studies and transportation planning projects has been the high degree of dependence on public transit by low-income persons. The 1960 U.S. Census found that 50 to 80 percent of transit riders in most large cities have a family income of under $4,000.[16] Despite this dependency, many areas where lower income persons are concentrated are not adequately served by existing transit systems. The conclusions to a study entitled *People, Jobs, and Transportation: An Examination of Transportation as a Factor in Oakland's Unemployment*, prepared by the City Planning Department of Oakland, California provides one example:

Inadequate public transportation limits the range of employment opportunities to unemployed West Oakland residents by adding time and cost barriers to job seeking and commuting. An increasing number of the East Bay's relatively available, traditionally male, blue collar jobs are so far from West Oakland (e.g., Southern Alameda County industrial parks) or so poorly served (e.g., Oakland

Airport), that a car is required for both job hunting or commuting. This is compounded by continued patterns of housing and employment discrimination which lead more Negroes than any other group to live in Oakland and commute out to jobs elsewhere, and by the fact that West Oakland has the lowest degree of car availability in the city. Such transportation barriers probably inhibit job hunting by the qualified, add further obstacles to the hardcore unemployed, and constrain operations of the various current publicly supported programs for basic education, job training, job placement, supportive service and anti-discrimination.[17]

George Evans, Director of Planning for Westmoreland County, Pennsylvania, during a speech made June 8, 1970, explained that due to curtailment of commuter service by both the Penn Central and nine of the ten privately-owned bus companies operating within the county, there was virtually no way that metropolitan Pittsburgh's population of semiskilled and unskilled workers without an available car could have access to the employment opportunities available at the new Chrysler auto assembly plant in New Stanton or the industrial area of the Turtle Creek in Allegheny County.[18]

Further, a study done by Alan M. Voorhees & Associates, Inc., in Nashville, Tennessee, also indicated that many jobs were not accessible by transit for the lower income communities. Surveys showed that while most jobs were found to be within 30 minutes travel time by automobile from a low-income area, less than a quarter of the jobs were within a half-hour travel time by transit and more than a quarter of the employment opportunities were totally inaccessible by public transit.

The high correlation between car ownership and income and the limited number of transit systems now providing adequate service to ghettos and concentrated areas of low-income persons has, in effect, created "... two societies—one served by auto and one served by public transportation, and the level of service is substantially different."[19] The problems and anger which have been generated by this disparity were voiced by the late Whitney Young, Jr., at the Fourth International Conference on Urban Transportation:

Since World War II, we've spent well over $50 billion on highways—50 times as much as has been spent on mass transit. If a city wants to build a highway, it can get the Federal Government to pay 90% of the cost; if it wants to build a subway, it has to beg for pennies. Much of the money for highways comes from gasoline taxes, but the cost to the city in terms of air and noise pollution, street upkeep, congestion and frayed nerves, is absorbed by the people who still live in the central cities. And increasingly that is coming to mean the poor and the black.

They don't own the cars. Four out of five white people own cars, but only half of the Negroes do. That also means the poor can't get to where the jobs are. Two thirds of all industrial buildings and half of all retail stores are going up in the suburbs. So we are faced with the strange situation of having labor shortages in the suburbs and unemployment in the urban ghettos. All this amounts to a massive failure on the part of the people who plan and set transportation policies in America.[20]

A quantitative example of the impact of equality of access by means of transit is shown in Table 1-1. The figures in this table represent estimates of the costs to society from lost production and increased welfare costs should bus lines serving Sacramento County go out of business. Adjustments were made for those people taken off welfare rolls and employed as a result of replacing other workers without personal transportation. It was assumed that one-half of the workers losing their jobs due to the discontinuation of the bus service would have family incomes from other sources (such as employed spouses, retirement, or investments), while others would have no source of income and would be forced to go on welfare. The estimate was that half of the persons affected would fall into the latter category. Cost was based on an average cost per welfare case, plus a 19.72 percent average administrative cost in Sacramento County. Lost wages were based on conservative estimates of $1.65 per hour and an average of four hours of work per day.

Table 1-1
Estimated Increased Welfare Costs and Loss in Wages for Captive Riders

Bus Line	Loss of Wages			Increase in Welfare		
	Peak	Off-Peak	Total	Peak	Off-Peak	Total
1	$ 73,125	$ 55,165	$128,290	$129,825	$ 97,938	$ 227,763
2	49,768	19,312	68,970	88,166	34,287	122,453
3	42,012	35,788	77,800	88,816	75,658	164,474
4	44,226	29,484	73,710	75,096	50,064	125,160
5	84,691	63,889	148,580	124,829	94,169	218,998
6	69,605	48,370	117,975	123,581	94,878	209,459
7	33,575	36,372	39,947	46,836	50,740	97,576
8	41,101	48,250	89,351	57,336	67,308	124,644
9						
10	8,072	1,206	9,278	21,037	3,144	24,181
11 } 12	30,866	13,229	44,095	70,920	30,394	101,314
13	6,722	7,890	14,612	14,586	17,123	31,709
14	14,514	14,513	29,027	23,137	23,137	46,274
15	20,290	19,495	39,785	27,807	26,717	54,524
16	2,513	2,140	4,653	6,543	5,573	12,116
17 } 18	17,318	18,025	35,343	22,548	23,469	46,017
19	825		825	1,289		1,289
Total	$539,113	$413,128	$952,241	$922,352	$694,599	$1,616,951

Source: Milton Baum, Albert Gutowsky, and Gerald Rucker, *Cost and Benefit Evaluation of the Sacramento Transit Authority*, Interim Technical Report #4, Sacramento State College, October 1970, p. 29.

Comparable figures on welfare cost savings and increased production resulting from extensions or development of transit systems were not available for use in this study. Nevertheless, increased ridership figures do provide some indication of this type of impact. For example, the Dan Ryan rapid transit extension which opened in Chicago in September 1970 connects a large black and low-income area of south and westside Chicago, and provides new rapid transit service in the section of the city south of 63rd Street that had no such service previously. Far exceeding original estimates of 30,000 riders per average weekday, the extension has averaged more than 70,000 riders daily.[21]

The effectiveness of new transit planning methodology in providing links through either new or expanded public transportation facilities to inner-city poverty areas are illustrated with specific examples in Part II of this study.

The Elderly and Youth

The elderly. Elderly Americans now number over 20 million—about one-tenth of the population—and their numbers have increased throughout the nation by approximately 14 percent over the last decade.[22] For persons 65 years and older, transportation, according to findings of the National Council on the Aging, is their second greatest problem, next to income.[23] The Council-sponsored Project FIND identified two principal reasons behind the frequency of transportation difficulties expressed by the elderly during a series of surveys:

1. Inadequate income is probably the foremost obstacle to adequate transportation for older persons. Almost a quarter of the population who are 65 and over live below the poverty level, established for purposes of the Social Security Administration poverty line. Inadequate income is a barrier not only to the ownership and operation of automobiles, but also to riding taxis or even to using some mass transit systems with ever rising fares.[24]
2. Many elderly persons suffer from impaired physical ability which precludes or makes hazardous the driving of automobiles.

These two reasons are so significant to the elderly that in most areas of the country persons 65 years of age or older rank first in numbers of transit riders by age group. Illustrative of this is Table 1-2 which summarizes the results of a study of transit riders in Albany, Savannah, Milwaukee, Columbus, Macon, and Augusta. Savannah was the only city where transit usage within the 65 and over age group was not highly significant, and according to the report, this was explained by the low levels of public transit service in Georgia cities.[25]

Other independent studies support these findings. For example:

A sampling of two public housing communities in Pittsburgh has shown that 90 percent of the elderly sampled have family incomes of less than $3,000 and

Table 1-2
Average Percentage of Trips Made by Transit for Six Selected Cities

	Work	Shop	Misc.	All Purposes
5-14	5.6	2.2	1.4	1.6
15-24	11.2	4.3	2.7	2.1
25-34	5.9	1.6	1.0	0.8
35-44	7.8	2.2	1.3	0.9
45-54	8.4	2.8	1.5	1.1
55-64	11.2	5.4	3.6	2.2
65 and over	11.3	8.2	6.9	2.7
Average all Ages	9.2	3.8	2.6	1.6

Source: Norman Ashford and Frank M. Holloway, "The Effect of Age on Urban Travel Behavior," *Traffic Engineering*, April 1971, p. 47.

approximately 85 percent have no available automobile. Upwards of 70 percent of all trips in both communities are made by bus.[26]

As part of its proposal to obtain a capital grant for the purchase of four new buses and auxiliary maintenance equipment, the City of Laguna Beach noted that a significant percentage of passengers (possibly as high as 80 to 90 percent) are 65 years or older and rely on mass transportation service for their daily mobility needs.[27]

Despite the elderly's relatively high usage and often complete dependence on transit for traveling to church or synagogue, shopping, medical facilities, health services, and even to participation in community programs at centers that are not within walking distance, the present state of transit equipment and service in many areas creates more problems than it solves. The National Council on the Aging has prepared a series of specific recommendations which it believes would eliminate these problems:

— Because the older person is usually living on a reduced, fixed income public transportation should be available at a price he can afford.
— The routing of public transportation should consider the needs and facilities available for older persons.
— The scheduling of service should recognize the limitations of older persons as well as the factors of weather and waiting time.
— The access to service (that is, stairs, ramps, height of steps, elevators, and so forth) are important to older persons, as well as the factors of weather and waiting time.
— Representatives on any committees to consider the details of urban mass transit should include older persons or representatives of organizations working with and for the elderly.[28]

The inadequacies of the existing transportation system alternatives effectively reduce the income of the elderly by introducing situations where ". . . lack of transportation keeps them from shopping at shopping centers so they could take advantage of lower prices. They have to buy from neighborhood stores which charge more for their products, and thereby the small amount of their incomes cannot be stretched to a full advantage."[29]

Reduction of transit fares in the City of New York has resulted in a 27 to 32 percent increase in usage by older persons.[30] On January 20, 1972, the *Washington Post* reported that, as a result of a reduced fare program during the past nine months, 10,000 to 20,000 persons over 65 years of age have been riding D.C. transit system buses during nonrush-hour workdays for 25 cents instead of the normal 40-cent fare. In Pittsburgh, it was learned that if better equipment and frequency of service were available, some 70 percent of the elderly who still drive to work would switch to transit, even if transferring between buses was required.[31] In one Project FIND area, the need for transportation was so great that an attempt was made to purchase cars and buses for the program by collecting trading stamps (2,200 books of stamps per car).[32]

Under Title III of the Older American Act of 1965, a project grant was given to the YMCA of Metropolitan Chicago to provide free minibus service to enable older persons with substantial transportation problems to take advantage of health, welfare, and recreational services from which they would otherwise be isolated. The conclusion of the demonstration program was that ". . . providing these transportation services had a significant therapeutic effect on the older people who were served, and . . . has helped give dejected, withdrawn older persons a new lease on life."[33]

Several conclusions can be drawn from the preceding data:

1. The elderly are the heaviest users of public transit.
2. The elderly depend on public transit to provide access to the basic necessities of life.
3. A large percentage of the elderly have no viable alternative to public transit.
4. The elderly would use public transportation more often if fares were lower, since their demand for such services is elastic; that is, as price declines, ridership increases.

Youth. Referring once again to the Ashford and Holloway six-city study, Table 1-2 shows that the second greatest percentage of transit trips were made by passengers in the 15-to-24-year-old age group. There has, however, been very little research and study into transit's impact on access opportunity for youth. The two cases described in the paragraphs which follow give evidence of how transit has been used to provide access to summer employment opportunities for youth from inner-city poverty areas.

During the summer of 1970 a Job Express Transportation (JET) demonstration project was initiated in the City of Baltimore to provide transit for youth from inner-city neighborhoods to centers of summer employment. The main target area was the office of the Social Security Administration which allocated slots for 400 summer aides. One problem was evident during prior summer employment programs, however—summer aides always experienced a long waiting period before receiving their first pay check, thus creating a hardship for those who still had to pay for their transportation during this period. In past summers, this situation resulted in high dropout and absenteeism rates. To alleviate this problem, a bus card system was set up under the JET program. The City of Baltimore agreed to purchase bus cards from the MTA, which gave the aides 40 trips or 20 days of free bus-riding privileges. The cards were valid on all MTA transit lines as well as on JET buses. Further, the issuance of the cards and distribution of route maps and schedules for all JET service to the Social Security Administration was administered by the JET staff. Extra bus service was also initiated by the JET staff to handle the later shifts at the Social Security Administration.

At the conclusion of the program, it was determined that of the summer aides who used public transportation to and from work, approximately 50 percent rode the JET buses, thus falling short of the original goal of 75 percent ridership. Of much greater significance was the fact that the absenteeism and dropouts of the summer aides showed a marked reduction over past summers.[34]

Another summer program during 1970, called Youth Opportunity '70, was launched in Columbus, Georgia. During the planning stages, it became evident that the major obstacle to the success of the program would be finding transportation to the scattered work sites. The ultimate solution to the problem was made possible as a result of an UMTA grant received in the fall of 1968. This grant, matched by city funds, was used for a $1 million purchase of new air-conditioned buses. During the winter months these were used along with the city's older buses. In the summer, however, reduced ridership levels meant that the newer, air-conditioned buses were sufficient to handle the daily passenger flow, so the city arranged for the older buses to be used for the Youth Opportunity Program, both to train drivers and to transport some 600 youths (507 of these from the black community) to and from job sites. Counted in terms of the four-trip split, the buses transported a total of 1,200 persons per day.[35]

The Ashford study concluded that "in the highest and lowest age groups there is a large proportion of riders who are captive to the transit mode. At low levels of transit service, it can be assumed that a significant number of trips remain unmade, giving a high latent demand for transportation."[36]

The significance of the latent demand for inexpensive and reliable means of mobility by the youth of even a relatively affluent community has been underscored by a minibus demonstration project in the Town of Hempstead on

Long Island, New York. Whereas the primary objective of the partially UMTA-sponsored project was directed toward generating a viable level of commuter ridership to and from a local New York City-bound railroad station, the unexpected findings at the conclusion of the two-year project pointed to the substantial potential ridership by the youths. The low-density residential pattern of this middle- to high-income family community did not lend itself to developing maximum use of this particular minibus program. On the other hand, the ridership by the young during nonschool hours turned out to be substantial, and the Saturday ridership averaged 137.4 percent of seat utilization, consequently resulting in a continuation of this portion of service by the local bus company subsequent to the termination of the project.[37] (See the Dial-A-Ride section in Chapter 5.)

The elimination of the need for reliance on private automobiles could significantly reduce the financial burden for college student and vocational trainees, as well as facilitate accessibility to a greater number of cultural, educational, and social opportunities that interest them. A prime example of a transit system which will benefit college students is the BART system of San Francisco, which is expected to almost eliminate the automobile requirement by students. Most of the area's colleges and vocational institutions will be conveniently serviced by the BART system. Moreover, the economic benefit will be particularly substantial to some 20,000 students enrolled at Laney College and City College of San Francisco, both of which provide vocational and academic training to students of low-income background. In addition, some 27,000 students at the University of California at Berkeley and numerous night- and part-time attendants of specialized vocational training facilities in the city will also be beneficiaries. (See the section on the San Francisco Bay Area Rapid Transit System in Chapter 4.)

The Handicapped

As defined by the National Center for Health Statistics, the chronically handicapped are those who have one or more long-term diseases which are included on the Checklist of Chronic Conditions or who have had any disease or impairment for more than three months. Three percent of the population—more than six million—fall within this category. It is anticipated that over the next 15-year period, increases of more than 40 percent of the current population will experience heart disease impairment of the upper and lower limbs, and visual defects.[38]

Many handicapped persons also are in the elderly and/or poor categories, the latter often due to the fact that access to employment opportunities is one of their most significant problems. It has been estimated that only about 36 percent of the national handicapped population between the ages of 17 and 64 are members of the labor force, compared with 71 percent of the nonhandicapped population of the same age group. Of a sample taken in metropolitan Pittsburgh, 52 percent of the handicapped people had family incomes of less than $3,000, 84 percent less than $5,000, and only 3 percent greater than $10,000.[39]

Dependency on public transportation by handicapped persons who are employed is relatively high. Again citing from the Pittsburgh case, 77 percent of the handicapped use either a bus or a streetcar to get to work.[40]

A study by Abt Associates found that for 30 percent of the handicapped persons actively seeking employment, inadequate transportation was considered the principal obstacle to finding a job.[41] Assuming that only the handicapped persons located in SMSAs would be likely to benefit, the study team estimated that a metropolitan transportation program designed to help the handicapped throughout the nation could return 189,000 people to work. Employment of this group at salary levels equal to those prior to their disability could further result in total yearly economic benefits of more than $824 million.[42]

The Carnegie-Mellon survey found that the problems associated with existing transit systems which posed the most difficulty for the handicapped were related to service and schedule difficulties. Another study conducted by Alan Voorhees indicated that 41 percent of inner-city dwellers who had to travel for medical purposes required mode changes as compared to 19 percent who traveled for work.[43]

Among new transit developments which should have a favorable impact on transportation of the handicapped is the new design for rapid rail cars, such as will be used for the BART and WMATA systems. Plans for this new equipment call for better planning of internal space to reduce crowding conditions, doorways designed to provide ease of access for the physically disabled, and sophisticated braking and propulsion systems to eliminate jarring and jerking motions as the trains start and stop.

Another example of innovation in meeting the transit needs of the handicapped is described below:

The following is a sample list of techniques we [UMTA] will demonstrate to inform the blind and deaf of transit services: (1) loud speaker systems at subway stations that announce routes and cars to take to destination; (2) loud speakers on buses that announce stops in advance of stop; (3) bus shelters equipped with demand actuated speakers which announce bus schedules and routes from that stop; (4) trip maps which indicate where traveler is and how he gets to destination; shows transfer points both intra and inter modal; shows total cost of trip; and, prints out directions; (5) a braille schedule and map available at information centers and mailed to blind people; (6) use of symbols, colors, and extra large lettering to describe routes, both on buses and transit stations; and, personal mailing to elderly to describe transit systems using lists from senior citizen centers, medicare, and other organizations.[44]

Summary

The preceding pages have reviewed the transportation needs of the potential of public transit to meet legitimate demands for access to basic necessities and urban opportunities. Implicit in this section is the concept that equality of access is essential to the promotion of greater social and economic equity for the more than 52 million poor, elderly, and/or handicapped persons who are captive riders, solely dependent on public transit for mobility.

The need for better public transit is underscored by the fact that many of the poor, the elderly, and the handicapped are concentrated in our central cities. More than 60 percent of the poor reside in central cities, as do 55 percent of those 65 and over. A quarter of the country's 65 and older group also have annual family incomes of $3,000 and under. Of the handicapped people, 52 percent have family incomes of less than $3,000. Of the households with incomes under $3,000, 46 percent, and more than half of all black families, do not own cars. As a result, 50 to 80 percent of total transit ridership in metropolitan areas is composed of poor persons.

Public transit can also have several beneficial impacts—direct and indirect—with respect to these segments of the population. It can open up ghetto areas to employment, educational, cultural, and recreational opportunities, as evidenced by the success of the Dan Ryan rapid transit extension in Chicago. It can provide access to new sources of income as well as lower welfare payments, as much as $53,113 and $1,616,951 respectively in the case of Sacramento.

In addition to the foregoing, an efficient rapid transit system can also mean better access to essential health and medical facilities for the elderly and the handicapped, but only if rates are kept within reason. For the youth, it can result in transportation to summer jobs and welfare and vocational programs, in addition to providing access to cultural activities and increasing social contacts.

Time Savings

Time savings to commuters diverted from automobiles to public rapid transit have several origins:[a]

1. Special rights of way and regulated headways eliminate problems of congestion.
2. Modern rapid transit systems travel at higher speeds than automobiles.
3. Rapid rail systems generally are unaffected by adverse weather conditions or

---

[a]The time savings discussed are those accruing to transit users diverted from automobile transportation. Time-saving benefits to other travelers due to less highway congestion from diversion are examined in Part II of this volume.

delays as is the case with automobile breakdowns or highway accidents tying up major arteries during rush-hour peaks.

The potential of rapid transit for increasing time savings is widely recognized. For example, during an opinion survey on the proposed Atlanta rapid transit system (MARTA), out of 1,043 respondents more than three quarters (76.9 percent) of the persons interviewed were in favor of a rapid transit system in Atlanta. Their primary reasons for supporting the proposal were to relieve traffic congestion and shorten travel time.[45]

Attempts have been made to measure quantitatively the benefit of time savings. One approach utilizes the "compensating variation in income" measure which focuses on the minimum amount of money a passenger requires to compensate him for an adverse change in travel times. This provides a rough dollar measure of the cost to the passenger of schedule delays or changes in travel time due to the use of the alternative transportation modes.[46]

Illustrative of efforts to measure the impact of time savings is the Baum, Gutowsky, and Rucker cost benefit analysis of the Sacramento Transit System. In this study, the value of a person's time was estimated to range from $1.55 to $3.75 per hour. Under the assumptions used in the study, the total benefits for the transit were calculated to exceed costs within a range of $2,660,999 to $3,912,090 based on value of time utilized.[47] Using a reverse approach, Baum, Gutowsky, and Rucker also estimated the costs of time lost for several levels of time values (see Table 1-3) resulting from the alternatives for the elimination of transit service by various bus lines.

In its cost-benefit analysis of the proposed five-corridor rapid transit system for Los Angeles, the Stanford Research Institute (SRI) used as the value of time $2.82 per person per hour.[48] Its estimates on the monetary equivalent of time savings for the nation's third largest city exceeded $38 million during the first full year of operation of the proposed rapid transit system. The SRI calculations included a cost deduction for time lost during the system's construction period.

The values of time savings discussed in the previous paragraph are derivatives of the elimination of the congestion factor and improved speed of transit versus automobiles. Additional examples of time savings can be found in the case studies included under Part II of this volume.

Another source of time savings from the use of rapid transit is a result of uninterrupted service during periods of bad weather. A series of investigations by Development Research Associates (DRA) produced evidence that there is a strong correlation between bad weather and decreases in over-the-road commutation. A survey of Chicago, New York, and Philadelphia by DRA found that ridership on rail transit in these cities increases by an average of 15 percent during inclement weather.[49] For the Washington, D.C., metropolitan area, DRA also has estimated the potential annual benefits of the new rapid transit system in eliminating early dismissal due to bad weather. Using a simple

Table 1-3

Estimated Increased Congestion Costs to Automobile Users from Elimination of Transit During Peak Only

Bus Line	Values of Time			
	1.55*	$1.80*	$2.80*	$3.75*
1	71,408	84,391	110,358	175,275
2	70,896	83,786	109,567	174,018
3	50,120	59,233	77,458	123,021
4	31,378	37,083	48,494	77,020
5	46,963	55,507	72,579	115,272
6	95,804	113,223	148,060	235,155
7	24,813	29,324	38,347	60,904
8	32,872	38,853	50,808	80,695
10**	--	--	--	--
11 }12	95,585	112,968	147,722	234,617
13	123,558	160,232	209,532	332,788
14	72,914	86,171	112,685	178,970
15	59,110	69,858	91,352	145,089
16	37,755	44,619	58,348	92,670
17 }18	26,656	31,503	41,196	65,429
19**	--	--	--	--
	839,832	1,006,751	1,316,508	2,090,923

*Value per hour per person.

**Line 10 carried so few passengers that congestion costs if automobiles were substituted would be insignificant.

***Line 19 did no travel on the highly congested roads or arterials.

Source: Milton Baum, Albert Gutowsky, and Gerald Rucker, *Cost and Benefit Evaluation of the Sacramento Transit Authority*, Interim Technical Report #4, Sacramento State College, October 1970, p. 24.

historical average of hours lost to early dismissal (four hours), DRA estimated that the annual benefits in 1990 will approximate $3,995 million.

In sum, the use of time savings as a measure of relative economies of various modes of transit stems from the relation of productive use of time to total economic efficiency. The information presented above thus clearly demonstrates the relative economic efficiency of rapid transit over alternate modes, whether measured in terms of lost production (the value-*of*-a-person approach) or in terms of reduced productivity (the value-*to*-a-person approach).

In summary, many of the nation's newly implemented public transit systems have attained sizable time savings for their patrons, as compared to the time required by automobile driving or previously available public transit means. Shorter travel time is often the most immediate reason that people are diverted to public transit ridership. Furthermore, diversion to transit directly contributes to shorter travel time for those who, through preference or need, continue to drive; they benefit through reduced congestion and improved traffic flow on freeways and city streets, particularly during the peak-load periods.

Rapid transit systems make possible time savings in still another area—that is, their travel time generally remains unaffected during bad weather conditions. Experience in Chicago, New York, and Philadelphia indicates that on days of inclement weather, rapid rail ridership increases as much as 15 percent. The rapid transit mode is also free of the delays and uncertainties which afflict over-the-road travelers in cases of accidents and automobile breakdowns.

Cost Savings Related to Vehicle Ownership and Operation

The opportunity for substantial savings in automobile ownership and operating costs—for both transit and nontransit travelers—exists when the alternative of rapid transit is available. For transit riders, these savings result from (i) a reduction in the number of cars needed per household, (ii) reduction in the amount of gas, oil, maintenance, and tires needed, and (iii) a reduction in parking costs. Operating savings also accrue to nontransit riders who continue to use automobiles, but who encounter less delay in traffic; thus, their vehicles are subject to less wear and tear and lower consumption of gas and oil. Finally, savings in parking costs are a benefit to automobile users who no longer use a car or who use one only to reach the transit station, but who can park there toll free or at lower cost.

A study by SRI investigated the potential reduction in the total number of motor vehicles needed when the alternative of rapid transit was made available, based on an analysis of the predicted increase in multicar households for the years between 1960 and 1980.[50] The resulting decrease in ownership costs (including depreciation, insurance, and registration fees), assuming that one-tenth of potential vehicle reduction would occur, was calculated to be $3.4 million annually. Other estimates indicate that the purchase of a new $3,000 car actually involves a total expenditure on the part of the owner of $11,000 over 10 years including gas, oil, insurance, maintenance, and repairs, tolls and parking fees, tires, and taxes.[51]

In terms of operating cost savings, a typical BART passenger is expected to save 50 cents on a round trip, compared to auto travel ($1.80 versus $1.30).[52] A detailed comparison for various trips to the CBD by automobile and transit was developed for the St. Louis area (see Table 1-4 for the results). Automobile costs

Table 1-4

Long-Range Transit Program, Comparison of Trip Costs to St. Louis Central Business District

Trip Origin	Distance to CBD (miles)	Daily Automobile Cost	Daily Transit Cost
West End	4	$1.77	$0.60
Holly Hills	5	1.85	0.70
Kinloch	10	2.24	1.20
Floussant	14	2.55	1.60
Clayton	7	2.00	0.90
Kirkwood	13	2.48	1.50
Affton	8	2.08	1.00
Mehlville	12	2.40	1.40
St. Charles	21	3.11	2.30
Ballwin	20	3.03	2.20
Arnold	19	2.95	2.10
Granite City	7	2.00	0.90
Collinsville	11	2.32	1.30
Belleville	14	2.55	1.60
Columbia	15	2.64	1.70
Alton	21	3.11	2.30
Edwardsville	23	3.27	2.50

Source: Parsons, Brinckerhoff, Tudor, Bechtel, Sverdrup & Parcel, *St. Louis Metropolitan Area: Rapid Transit Feasibility Study, Long-Range Program*, PB204-060, St. Louis, August 1971, p. 82.

were based on out-of-pocket costs at $.395 per mile, round-trip mileage, and a nine-hour parking cost of $1.45. Out-of-pocket cost per mile was derived for an eight-cylinder, automatic transmission car driven 10,000 miles a year. Costs included gas, oil, maintenance, and tire replacement, but excluded insurance, depreciation, and license fees.

The St. Louis study further cites possible cost savings for automobile insurance premiums of $20.40 a year for a married male over 25 years of age, who drives a medium priced two-year-old car and lives within 10 miles of his job. Another similar study estimating potential vehicle savings by switching to transit commuting was conducted for Los Angeles (see Table 1-5).[53] Included in the total annual savings are benefits to commuters who continued driving to work on highways and local streets that were less congested as a result of the new transit installation. Vehicle operating costs in the Los Angeles study included fuel, oil, maintenance, parts, and labor, varying with number of miles driven. Depreciation, registration, and part of insurance costs were excluded, since these categories were classified under vehicle ownership cost savings. (Insurance costs

Table 1-5
Total Savings in Vehicle Operating Costs by Use of Rapid Transit

A. Savings for rapid transit patrons diverted from automobiles.

Type of Facility	Daily Reduction in Vehicle Miles Driven (1,000's)	Cost Per Vehicle Mile ($)	Total Cost Savings Daily ($1,000's)	Total Cost Savings Annual ($million)
Freeway	2,763.0	$.030	$ 82.9	$21.1
Arterial and local streets	4,464.9	.056	82.0	20.9
Total savings from rapid transit			$164.9	$42.0

B. Savings for motorists who continue to travel by automobile.

Type of Facility	Total Cost Savings Daily ($1,000's)	Total Cost Savings Annual ($million)
Freeway	$ 18.2	$ 4.6
Arterial and local streets	4.7	1.2
Total savings for remaining motorists	$ 22.9	$ 5.8

C. Dis-savings for motorists during construction period.

	Total Cost Savings —	Total Cost Savings Annual ($million)
Equivalent annual cost of additional vehicle operating costs		$−1.3
Total operating costs saved annually		$46.5

Source: SRI, University of California, *Reduction of Robberies and Assaults of Bus Drivers*, California, December 1970, p. 16.

were divided into two categories—liability and collision insurance costs, and fire and theft insurance cost; the latter were discussed under ownership costs.)

Further benefits possible through reduction of parking costs include the elimination of any parking cost if a car that used to be parked for a fee is no longer used or is parked at the transit station toll free, and savings from difference in parking payments between the transit station and the more expensive CBD parking facility. Parking costs potentially saved in the city of St. Louis were illustrated in the example given above which placed the nine-hour daily cost at $1.45 per car. Estimates on savings attributable to the BART system have included parking charges valued at nearly 7 percent of the total savings in vehicle operating costs.[54]

An indirect benefit which may result from diversion of commuters to public transit is lower insurance premiums. Reduced insurance rates may result from a decrease in the number of automobile accidents, as discussed in the next section of this chapter, as well as from less car thefts due to a smaller number of cars being parked on the streets or parking lots in the center city. For example, in 1971 there were 930,000 automobiles stolen throughout the country, a fact which has had substantial impact in reinforcing already rising auto insurance costs.[55]

In summary, savings in vehicle ownership, operating, and parking costs represent substantial potential benefits to automobile users who switch to rapid transit; estimates for various cities show that potential annual ownership savings would amount to $335 for each car no longer needed. For 5-mile, 10-mile, and 20-mile one-way trips, potential daily round-trip savings for those cars not used for daily commutation (including savings in parking costs) are calculated at $1.15, $1.04, and $.83 respectively—or annual savings of $276, $250, and $199.

Motorists may also benefit from instituting transit service. Reduction in the number of automobiles on highways and city streets, due to diversion to transit, produces better traffic flow and in turn reduced oil and gas consumption, as well as better running conditions for the machines. Finally, an indirect benefit to both transit passengers and motorists may come in the form of lower insurance premiums due to less car thefts from reduced inner city parking and fewer accidents.

Increased Safety

There are two aspects to consider in connection with increased safety—safety from accidents and safety from crime. Since statistics and other information regarding assaults and robberies of passengers are limited, the major portion of this section is devoted to a discussion of safety from accidents. An expanded presentation of safety from crime with respect to operators and drivers may be found in Chapter 2.

Criminal attacks on public transit users primarily receive periodical attention in such cities as New York or Philadelphia. New York installed special transit patrol forces to forestall attacks both on users and on transit personnel, especially fare-booth operators, and Philadelphia's program to improve subway station lighting and platform facilities aims at reducing criminal assaults (see the Philadelphia case study in Part II). Both programs resulted because old and poorly lighted stations with remote platform areas lent themselves to crime. Newer rapid transit systems, however, stress open, well-lighted and well-accessed stations, and the use of electronic surveillance equipment minimizes the likelihood of attacks. Data to contrast the incidence of crimes committed under different station conditions with the level of assaults suffered by the nontransit riding public are not available.

Accident cost savings related to the use of public transit are in part a function of the reduction in vehicle-miles driven, and in part a function of the fact that transit service is unusually accident-free compared with automobile use. In terms of fatalities alone, automobile travel is one of the most dangerous modes of movement. Each year, approximately 55,000 people are killed in highway and automobile accidents, averaging more than 150 lives lost each day.[56] Per hundred million miles traveled, there are 5.3 automobile fatalities, compared to .19 bus fatalities and 0.07 passenger train fatalities.[57]

Accident figures are equally impressive in magnitude and contrast. For example, in 1967 the total cost of the nation's traffic accidents, in terms of cash expenditures only, reached $12.5 billion. This is 1.5 percent of the GNP in 1967, or three times the budget for the U.S. Atomic Energy Commission or NASA. The annual rate of increase in the last years averaged about 10 percent.[58] Further, in 1970 approximately two million people were injured seriously in automobile accidents. The social costs in terms of human suffering are immeasurable.

In contrast to the automobile accidents, a recent press release issued by the Institute for Rapid Transit announced that in 1971, while operating 422,218,204 passenger car miles, rapid transit had the extremely low accident rate of .1113 accidents per million car miles of revenue operations. This accident rate becomes truly impressive with the realization that more than one and one-half billion people used rapid transit in 1971.[59]

The safety record of bus transit, while not as spectacular as rapid rail, still ranks substantially higher than automobiles. In 1962 the Chicago Transit Authority used a figure of 0.4¢ per passenger-mile as the cost of settling accident claims for bus traffic, and a cost of 0.1¢ per passenger-mile was used as the basis of settling accident claims for grade-separated rapid transit lines.[60]

In the years ahead the use of automatic control functions, such as are being planned for the BART and WMATA systems, should increase the safety record of rapid transit to all-time highs. As a result, and as increasing numbers of people are diverted from automobiles to new and improved rapid transit systems, an indirect benefit in the form of lower insurance premiums may be experienced.

The National Safety Council publishes information indicating that the vast majority of traffic fatalities occur within a short distance of the car occupants' homes. Since more than 70 percent of the nation's population is concentrated in urban areas, it becomes evident that urban populations may be undergoing needless exposure to death and injury by the use of automobiles. The high incidence of fatalities near home suggests that for urban dwellers with access to rapid transit, the risk of death could be reduced drastically by substitution of rapid transit for automobile travel, particularly where urban populations reach a concentration of 14,000 to 20,000 persons per square mile.[61]

In summary, the preceding pages have pointed strongly to the fact that public transit is capable of maintaining an extremely high safety record when contrasted to the record for private automobiles. On a passenger-mile-traveled basis, fatalities from automobile accidents are approximately 75 times greater than for passenger trains. Similarly, in 1971, rapid transit had an average of one accident per 30 million rides. This is a record of safe service no automobile service could be expected to achieve.

The social costs of automotive safety, both in terms of accidents and increased cost to the auto purchaser for safety devices, means that—based solely upon the safety criteria—automobiles rank much lower in economic efficiency than rapid rail. Although unable to match the record of the rail rapid mode, buses, too, offer a safer means of travel than private automobile.

2

Operator Benefits

Operation Cost Savings

Operator benefits that generally result from improvements in existing rapid transit systems and new technology involve reduction in operation and maintenance costs. Operating costs, for example, are reduced by increasing the speed and utilization of vehicles and also by reducing the crew required to operate them. Automation is the key to this latter benefit. Reductions in maintenance largely result from improvements in equipment design, such as larger and more efficient propulsion units that require less downtime and provide longer service life between maintenance and overhaul; the introduction of stainless steel cars which clean easily and do not require painting; automatic car cleaning equipment; and so forth. Table 2-1 shows a partial breakdown of total operating costs for two relatively new rapid transit systems as compared with the national average. Costs for the MBTA system in Boston are presented as well; these demonstrate the excessive costs resulting from antiquated equipment and systems.

The most overwhelming operating cost savings have been realized in construction through use of new systems which employ the latest technology, such as the Bay Area Rapid Transit in San Francisco, the Delaware River Port Authority (DRPA), and the Philadelphia-Lindenwold rapid transit line. For example, the Philadelphia-Lindenwold is equipped with central computer control, requiring

Table 2-1
Comparison of the Cost Per Car Mile of Systems Operations for the Cleveland, San Francisco, and Boston Rapid Transit Systems*

	Cleveland (CTS)	San Francisco (BART)**	Boston***
Service Operations	.57	.42	.96
Maintenance	.35	.33	.41
Administration	.27	.27	.35
TOTAL Operating Cost per Passenger Mile	$1.19	$1.02	$1.72

*Average for other major national systems as surveyed by BART planners is $1.32 per car-mile.

**San Francisco figures are projected to the first year of full operations in 1975.

***1966 figures, indicating the cost inefficiency resulting from old equipment.

only three men during operating hours; automatic train operations, requiring only one motorman in a passive role; and automatic fare collection at stations, requiring virtually no station attendants. Thus an approximate 70 percent reduction in operating and administrative staff—from 775 for older lines serving comparable areas to 225 for the Lindenwold line—has been achieved.

In Boston, the Massachusetts Bay Transportation Authority purchased new high-speed transit cars for its Cambridge-Ashmont line in 1964. Both faster and more reliable, 92 of these cars satisfy the same service requirements of 135 older ones. Much of the reason for the reduction in fleet size with new equipment is reduced maintenance, and, therefore, reduced downtime requirements. The DRPA, for instance, requires only five spare cars in its initial fleet of 75, while the older fleet of 135 on the Cambridge-Ashmont line in Boston had an average of 20 in the shops or undergoing routine maintenance. In addition, more powerful motors and automatic train operations have reduced round-trip travel times resulting in greater overall utilization. It was estimated that a savings of three minutes in average running time for a 29-mile round trip is equivalent to adding one extra train to in-service operations. This is beneficial not only because it increases speed and frequency of service and eliminates the need for one extra train, but it also eliminates an extra crew. In a simulation study done for the MBTA, what is now considered low-performance rapid transit cars (top speed 65 mph, rate of acceleration of 2.4 mphps[a]) was compared with high-performance cars (top speed 75 mph, rate of acceleration 3.0 mphps); it was found that a route with 13 two-car trains with low-performance propulsion equipment would cost $56,000 per year more for equipment and over $1 million more for crew than if the same system employed the high-performance equipment. Likewise, the new systems are more reliable to operate because of computer scheduling, and the automatic control of train movements is safer because of the greater redundancy in signaling, braking, and elaborate hazard detection subsystems. They also are more efficient, having a capability of responding to overloads and emergency conditions in an on-line manner.

Automatic car identification (ACI) systems—which are just coming into service in yards and at transfer blocks to identify cars, determine mileage, location, and direction, and transmit those data to the central control computer—have provided labor savings and efficiency in car inventory and maintenance scheduling functions. ACI, for example, is being used in the BART system specifically to aid in the automatic balancing of car storage, maintenance, utilization, and record keeping. For BART, this device should have at least one full-time man when the system is in full swing.

Automatic coupling systems also have saved in operating costs. Where it previously required two extra men for each coupling operation at the transfer or terminal block, with automatic couplers, the motorman can effectively perform the coupling operation himself.

---

[a]Miles per hour per second, in terms of acceleration.

Computer simulation of train operation and scheduling programs implemented in systems similar to those in San Francisco and New York eliminate, at minimum, scheduling errors and inefficiencies and, in some cases, the need for extra dispatchers.

Closed-circuit television installed for surveillance of stations has improved platform security and helped discourage incidents of crime and vandalism. In addition, automatic fare collection equipment in stations has eliminated the need for change clerks and, in some cases, station attendants. Further, it has also provided the opportunity to effectively implement heretofore unmanageable graduated fare systems based on mileage—an advantage that will facilitate the building of regional extensions.

Another new development which, when implemented, will benefit operations by reducing costs is the use of high voltage alternating current in train propulsion systems. This will reduce the overall cost of system power by reducing transmission, transformer, and rectification costs. Likewise, new propulsion equipment makes more efficient use of electric power.

In summary, improvements in existing systems as well as the installation of new rapid transit systems can result both in lowered operation and maintenance costs. New equipment units can travel safely at higher speeds, thereby reducing the number of units needed to service a route. Commensurate reductions in the number of crews are also possible. Since many functions in the new vehicles are controlled automatically, the size of crews is also smaller. In Boston, one study dealing with the use of new equipment on a route showed possible equipment savings of $56,000 and labor savings of $1 million per year. Besides direct operating savings, many ancillary operations are able to be automated, including car inventory, maintenance scheduling, coupling, dispatching, and fare collection systems, thus further eliminating opportunities for errors.

Maintenance Cost Savings

Transit operators have experienced a significant reduction in the maintenance costs of new systems for several reasons. These include (i) better equipment with better design, greater overall capacity to absorb overloads, and longer service life; (ii) better control over maintenance procedures with regard to scheduling routine maintenance in a more balanced manner; (iii) more sophisticated testing devices as well as more frequent testing; (iv) modular construction of equipment that requires maintenance, and automatic equipment for performing that maintenance; (v) better control over operations whereby damage maintenance and equipment losses are reduced; and (vi) larger cars with better overall utilization to reduce the average fleet size.

In 1962, the Southeastern Pennsylvania Transit Authority initiated a program to upgrade commuter service on six suburban Philadelphia commuter lines.

Initially they purchased 75 high-performance stainless steel multiple-unit Silver-liners and 12 rail diesel cars as part of a new fleet of 144 cars that would eventually replace more than 200 cars over 50 years old. The new cars were larger, faster, and easier to maintain, and required a smaller overall fleet size. Initial studies showed that the operating companies to whom the new cars were leased would save $9,105 per car in maintenance costs. This figure, combined with the smaller fleet required to service the lines, resulted in a projected annual savings of $1.3 million in annual maintenance costs alone.

BART in San Francisco predicts it will have one of the lowest-per-mile maintenance costs in the country, largely due to routine testing and checking procedures and modular construction of transit vehicles. BART cars will operate in three-car trains in which each car, having a special function in the overall train operation, will have a unique set of equipment. Therefore, duplication of equipment—especially electronic—is eliminated and fewer failures should be experienced. Furthermore, car design is such that each equipment subsystem failure, once detected, can be replaced temporarily by a spare unit. For example, if there is a failure in the onboard ATO equipment, the whole ATO unit will simply be replaced in modular fashion, thereby reducing overall car downtime. In many cases, this replacement can be performed right on the terminal block or in a lay-up track adjacent to the terminal. Larger jobs, such as the replacement of a truck or propulsion unit, must be done in a shop; but the job would also be accomplished by a simple replacement.

BART, as well as the new WMATA system, will have simple automatic failure checks each time a train is put into service. This is performed by the dispatcher, who plugs a test device into the train's electronic system which then runs a comprehensive check on all electrical systems. Error or failure readings will result in immediate replacement. In contrast, trains on older systems sometimes run for days before failures or overloads are detected, compounding the eventual problem and cost.

Routine maintenance such as car washing will be scheduled and performed automatically to reduce manpower requirements and increase efficiency. More-over, the stainless steel transit cars to be used require less exterior maintenance than older vehicles.

Testing of track for potential broken rail will, in the future, have a tremendous impact on maintenance and operating costs. Through electronic sounding devices, it is now possible to detect weak spots, and, therefore, potential failure points in rail long before broken rail is a danger. This testing is now provided by companies on a contractual basis. It is believed that a systems check on rail is only required once a year to ensure safe rail conditions. The implications of this technique are far-reaching. Designers of signal systems still cling, although reluctantly, to the concept of using costly track circuitry for establishing signal blocks. Track circuits in the signal system ensure that all operations are stopped should a rail separation occur. In some ways this is an archaic throwback to days when railroad people believed broken rail to be the line's biggest single hazard. Currently, however, there exist means by which fail-safe signaling can be done very cheaply and easily between trains by using space waves. Once acceptance of the fact that ultrasonic testing for broken rail, and the construction of the rail itself, are fail-safe, operating and maintenance costs for signal systems can be vastly reduced.

Wheels on the transit vehicle also can be tested ultrasonically for weak spots. This will be done automatically in the BART system. Likewise, wheel wear is automatically monitored, so that when wheels become irregular in shape or fall below a certain tolerance in size, they will be reground or replaced before serious maintenance is required.

In summary, then, direct maintenance cost savings are possible both because of the reduced number of units required in the new high-performance fleets and because of design features aimed at minimizing maintenance procedures and downtime. Modular units containing specialized equipment are to be used in the BART system cars, permitting simple replacement rather than removal of the complete car from service. Automated test devices also will be used to anticipate potential equipment failures and alleviate the cost of repairing eventually more serious damage, and similar testing will ultimately be possible for rail track.

Crime Prevention

General

Efforts to prevent crime on urban transportation systems focus largely on vandalism and personal attacks on rapid transit passengers and on robberies and assaults of bus drivers. The latter has received much recent attention because of the growing rate of assault and robbery on our national buses.

Methods of crime prevention in urban transit currently include:

1. Closed-circuit TV, emergency phones, improved lighting, and shorter platforms on rapid transit platforms.
2. Emergency telephones, alarms, and guards on transit cars.
3. Automatic fare collection equipment at rapid transit stations.
4. Exact fare systems and sealed fare boxes on buses.
5. Physical barrier between operators and passengers.

Crimes of vandalism, assault, and robbery in U.S. transit systems have grown at an alarming rate over the past few years. For instance, in a recent American Transit Association survey it was determined that, between 1963 and 1968, robberies of bus drivers had quintupled, and resulting injuries and fatalities to drivers had grown by over 1,000 percent. Table 2-2 shows, more specifically, the

Table 2-2
Increase in Robberies on Buses in Dade County, Florida

Year	Number of Robberies	Increase Over Prior Year	Increase Over Base Year
1965	18		
1966	13	(5)	(5)
1967	50	37	32
1968	185	135	157
1969	251	66	233

Source: Memorandum dated January 12, 1970, from R.A. Hauer, Resident Manager of the National City Management Company to Porter Homer, County Manager of Dade County, Florida.

statistics for Dade County (Miami), Florida, involving the growth of armed robberies in buses.

Evidence has also indicated that the threat to personal safety was sufficient to discourage some riders from using mass transportation facilities. The President's Commission on Law Enforcement and Administration of Justice, for example, found that the poor were particularly victimized, causing many to spend money on taxis because they were afraid to use public transportation. In a study of subway stations on Philadelphia's Broad Street subway, it was found that in six run-down, dark stations, patronage was actually falling while surface bus lines—which charged the same fare and traveled the same route—were overcrowded.

Benefits of Effective Countermeasures

User benefits. Users of public transit would benefit from effective countermeasures by decreased bodily harm, theft, and threat, reduced fear and apprehension about using the system, lower fares due to reduced system operating costs involved in repairing damage and fare-box losses. The most important benefit to passengers, however, is psychological. A passenger's whole perception of using rapid transit could be enhanced tremendously if he felt completely safe. During a Temple University study of subway improvements in Philadelphia, in which 600 subway riders were surveyed, it was found that safety was, by far, the largest single important factor to the average subway user.

In another survey by Keene Corporation on the benefits of the exact fare system on buses, the Wichita Metropolitan Transit Authority found that the loading time of buses had been cut by 20 percent.[1] This benefit was verified by other transportation authorities. During the same survey, it was found that the system also resulted in a more efficient operation and closer adherence to schedules in general.

Operator benefits. The most significant benefit of the countermeasures for operators has been in reduced losses due to robbery and vandalism. Elimination or reduction of vandalism on transit facilities is an important area for efforts to reduce the drain on operators' resources. For example, the Cleveland Transit System, which is considered to be in a much more favorable situation than others across the country, must spend about $16,000 a year to replace glass windows broken by rock throwing.[2] In addition, the system's 18 stations experienced 207 incidents of vandalism between October 1968 and April 1971.

The Keene Corporation survey concluded that there was virtually a 100 percent elimination of hold-ups aboard buses where the exact fare system was implemented.[3] In another survey of 212 cities, it was found that prior to the implementation of exact fare systems, the average bus driver robbery cost the system $101.[4] The commendable effect of the exact fare program is underscored by the overwhelming endorsement shown by almost every bus driver who participated in an SRI survey conducted during 1970.[5]

A strict security program carried out in the Lindenwold demonstration program has resulted in virtual absence of the problems of defacement and more serious vandalism. The TV monitor constantly scans the interior of all stations, and any person loitering is immediately spotted. The authority operating the line maintains a police department, headquartered in Broadway station, which consists of 19 men and four dogs. A man and a dog ride the late-night train, and police cars patrol the line and the parking lots. Train phones, call-for-aid phones, station phones, and mobile radios are the means by which passengers reach the police.

Summary

In response to the growing problems of vandalism, assault, and robbery, bus and rapid transit operators have introduced selective countermeasures which inhibit crime. Just as users benefit through decreased attacks and improved sense of personal safety, operators can realize sizable savings through lowered costs associated with crime.

Transit operators have virtually eliminated losses due to bus holdups by implementing exact fare systems and locked fare boxes. A nearly complete curtailment of vandalism has resulted from equipping stations and trains along Philadelphia's new Lindenwold line with television scanning devices, emergency telephones, and special police patrols.

3   Community Benefits

Benefits to Nontransit Travelers

Traffic Flow

Increased use of public transit which diverts people from automobile travel will inevitably have a strong impact on motorists. Every 50 persons diverted to public transit represent a reduction of approximately 30 automobiles in the traffic stream, with a consequent easing of downtown traffic and parking congestion. Reduced congestion will produce a number of benefits, including better movement of goods to and from businesses, especially in downtown street areas where congestion at the rush hours limits truck access to many establishments. Great benefits will also accrue to establishments which are located outside of the CBD but which have special ties to other firms requiring many face-to-face contacts. Included in this category are garment buyers and manufacturers, data processing firms, pharmaceutical retailers, and financial institutions.[1]

The problem of inner-city congestion is brought into focus by a few relevant statistics. There are now 200 million Americans, and 80 percent of them live in urban areas. By the year 2000, it is estimated that there will be 300 million Americans, with 90 percent of them living in so-called urban areas.

In 1950, there were 40 million automobiles in the United States—52 percent of the families owned one, and 7 percent owned at least two. By 1967, there were 80 million automobiles, with 53 percent of the families owning one, and 25 percent owning at least two.[2] In 1967, almost 53 million of these automobiles were concentrated in urban areas.[3] Moreover, every 24 hours 16,000 new automobiles are registered and about 6,000 are retired, thus producing a net increase of 10,000 automobiles daily.[4]

As congestion continues to increase, the social costs multiply in many ways; for example, *McCall's Magazine* estimates that traffic delays cost its publication approximately $50,000 extra annually in drivers' pay, gas, and equipment. Further, when frustrations build up and the drivers get "up-tight," efficiency drops and accidents occur.[5]

Stanford Research Institute has estimated that the truckers in metropolitan Los Angeles would accrue $1.2 million in time savings if highway congestion were reduced due to the operation of a rapid transit system. This is just one example of the benefit of improved traffic flow resulting from the diversion of commuters to public transit. Table 3-1 summarizes the passenger capacities per lane of track in one direction for automobiles and various modes of public transit.

Access to Airport

Despite the development of faster and more efficient airplanes, today's air travelers are increasingly forced to spend a greater portion of their total travel time on ground access to and from airports. Air passenger peak ground traffic tends to coincide with the period of commuter rush hours on highways and arterial routes to and out of the city center. The need for securing large tracts of land away from concentrated areas for reasons of safety and noise places airports further and further away from locations where public transportation is readily available.

Recognizing the need to expedite ground transportation for air travelers, many of the nation's cities with major airports are attempting solutions of various kinds. However, provision of a direct and fast link between downtown and airport in order to bypass congested roads can often be a costly venture, and sometimes necessitates a less conventional mode such as monorail. If the service is designed to primarily benefit air passengers, however, the volume does not generate a large enough ridership to ensure economic viability, as is the case with the monorail to the Tokyo airport. A more practical solution at the present time for meeting the ground access requirements for air passengers is possible, as has been successfully demonstrated by the Cleveland transit system. Since 1968, the Hopkins airport has been linked with the downtown area through a four-mile extension of the rapid transit system. At a headway of 10 to 12 minutes, the service transports airport-destined or -originated passengers over the 12-mile distance between the CBD and the airport in 22 minutes, which compares favorably with the 30 minutes that is required by the auto during rush hours on the recently completed freeway.

The extension was originally estimated to generate about 2,000 riders a day; instead it now serves as many as 4,000 riders a day.[6] Of these riders, 57.6 percent are air passengers.[7] Further, the extension resulted in the decline of three other modes of transportation—private automobile (8.2 percent decline), taxi (26 percent decline), and limousine (46.6 percent decline).[8]

Survey results indicate that 35 percent of the air passengers with local origin or destination in the Cleveland CBD use the rapid transit. Those passengers who do not begin or terminate their trips in the CBD have options to transfer to or from the Shaker Heights rapid transit system or public buses.

Summary

A dramatic difference in carrying capacity suggests that many automobile travelers may eliminate needless delays on congested urban roads if a rapid transit alternative exists. From Table 3-1 it can be seen that under high capacity conditions one track of rapid rail transit can move nearly 11 times as many people per hour as one lane of freeway (based on 180 passengers per car for a six-car train with one-and-a-half-minute headways, and two passengers per automobile at 18-second headways).

Thus, by removing vehicles from the traffic stream and reducing congestion, remaining motorists can complete their trips faster with time-related cost savings. These individuals develop the choice of substituting longer headways for some of the potential improvement in speed, and thereby obtaining a greater degree of safety. Further, businesses dependent upon surface distribution of goods or services accrue substantial savings in drivers' pay, gas, and equipment, as well as a lower accident rate from traffic-induced tension and fatigue. Vital police, fire, and ambulance services can also be delivered with fewer delays and with attendant reduction in possible loss of human lives.

Finally, transit service benefits travelers through provision of convenient and reliable ground access to and from the airport. The Cleveland experience was cited here as a successful case in this area of public transit utility.

Impact on Employment

Impact of public transit on employment falls into two categories: employment made possible by the availability of public transit to bring people to work; and jobs created in the development, construction, and operation of the system. The following sections present information relating to both categories.

In any discussion of economic vitality, one must consider the various strengths of the links between the production and the consumption side of each economic sector. Further, there can be no argument that efficient flow among these links has a direct bearing on the economic efficiency of each sector. Inasmuch as urban transit systems provide the primary access link for a major input factor of both urban production and consumption (that is, labor), they must have a multiplier effect on the general economic vitality (since each producer-consumer has a multiplier effect).

For example, Stanford Research Institute has estimated that the ability of the metropolitan Los Angeles area to hold population will increase by 10 percent with the development of a new rapid transit system. As a consequence, the economy of the area would be larger, as in the case of greater retail sales. The SRI study includes the impact on retail sales not as a net benefit, but as an important internal transfer. Evidence of this type of impact was seen during a minibus demonstration project under a grant from the Federal Housing and Home Finance Agency. The project involved the operation of 14 minibuses along F Street in Washington, D.C., where merchants expressed the opinion that the service was helping to make them competitive with suburban shopping centers. The sponsors of the program had originally anticipated about 900,000 passengers during the first year, but the number hit the one-million mark in

Table 3-1
Passenger Capacities per Lane or Track in One Direction

Vehicle	Facility	Vehicles Or Trains per Lane or Track per Hour	Headway (min.)	Effective Capacity at Various Passengers per Vehicle			
				1.25	1.50	1.75	2.00
Private Automobile	City Street, Design Flow Rate	600	0.10	750	900	1,050	1,200
	City Street, Capacity	800	0.13	1,000	1,200	1,400	1,600
	Freeway, Design Flow Rate	1,500	0.04	1,875	2,250	2,265	3,000
	Freeway, Capacity	2,000	0.03	2,500	3,000	3,500	4,000
				Effective Passenger Capacity for Various Loading Ratios			
				75%	100%	125%	150%
Transit Bus (50 seats)	City Street	60	1.00	2,250	3,000	3,750	4,500
	City Street	90	0.67	3,375	4,500	5,625	6,750
	City Street or Freeway	120[a]	0.50	4,500	6,000	7,500	9,000
	Freeway	180[a]	0.33	6,750	9,000	11,250	13,500
	Freeway	240[a]	0.25	9,000	12,000	15,000	18,000
Bus Rapid Transit (Manual operation)	Busway, 50-seat buses	120	0.50	4,500	6,000	7,500	9,000
		240	0.25	9,000	12,000	15,000	18,000
		1,200[b]	0.05	45,000	60,000	75,000	90,000
Automated Bus Train	10-car train, 50-seat bus	20	3.00	7,500	10,000	12,500	15,000
		40	1.50	15,000	20,000	25,000	30,000

				Effective Passenger Capacity at Various Passengers per Car			
				100	120	150	180
Rail Rapid Transit Train	6-car train	20	3.00	12,000	14,400	18,000	21,600
		30	2.00	18,000	21,600	27,000	32,400
		40	1.50	24,000	28,800	36,000	43,200
	10-car train	20	3.00	20,000	24,000	30,000	36,000
		30	2.00	30,000	36,000	45,000	54,000
		40	1.50	40,000	48,000	60,000	72,000

Source: *Capacities and Limitations of Urban Transportation Modes*, Institute of Traffic Engineers, 1965 (except for Bus Rapid Transit and Automated Bus Train, which were calculated by Parsons, Brinckerhoff et al., in their St. Louis study).

Note: This table provides the elements necessary to determine the number of persons that may be accommodated per facility. Example of the number of persons carried in the peak direction on representative facilities are:

8-lane freeway 7,500 to 16,000 persons per hour.

2-track rail rapid transit with 6-car trains 12,000 to 43,000 persons per hour.

This table considers capacity only. A more complete comparison must consider demand and level of service which reflect convenience, flexibility of use, comfort, and many other factors.

[a]Capacity would be limited by design of bus turn outs and type of operation.

[b]Possible maximum if suitable terminal capacity off the busway can be provided.

seven months; and after ten months in operation, 1.4 million passengers had ridden the line. Five out of six of these riders were shoppers.[9] Increased retail activity resulting from the development of the BART system is described in the third section of this chapter.

Regarding access to employment centers, it is estimated that Los Angeles could reduce its monthly welfare roles by 4,200 people if rapid transit were made available,[10] in addition to reducing the feeling of ghetto isolation and the possibility of a second major riot in Watts.[11] Although the key input to some of the area's industry is the availability of large amounts of low-wage labor, the need to travel long distances to reach work, at significant expense levels, causes a decline in the quantity of low-wage labor available. This input can be provided by rapid transit. A specific example of projected industry impact is in the apparel manufacturing industry in Los Angeles. It has been estimated that the proposed rapid transit system in Los Angeles would increase by 60 percent the availability of labor for the apparel industry, thus ensuring its survival. More employment, furthermore, generates more income for consumption. Better transit means better access to retail stores. Both situations can stimulate retail sales and, perhaps, indirectly result in higher employment levels in that sector of the urban economy.

Moreover, the creation of a rapid transit system involves two basic areas of labor input. One is the RDT&E (research, development, testing, and evaluation) and hardware manufacturing component; the other is the actual construction of the system. Both segments employ different categories of labor—scientific, engineering, and production workers in the first instance, and architects and laborers in the latter case. While exact data on employment generation are not available, several cases can be cited to indicate the magnitude of this field. Currently, about 5,000 men with a weekly payroll of $1 million are employed in the construction of BART,[12] making BART one of the biggest contributors to the local economy. The employment projections for the construction of the Los Angeles rapid transit system indicate that an average of 5,300 jobs a year for seven years could be expected.[13] This represents approximately 50 percent of the unemployed construction workers, a significant impact.

The research and development phase of supplying hardware for transit systems has enormous employment potential, as is highlighted by the efforts of the large aerospace system contractors to enter this market.[14] In fact, one aerospace contractor, Rohr Corporation, has played a major role in developing new technology for the BART system. In terms of occupations other than R&D-related, the United States transit industry, as a whole, employed approximately 138,000 people in 1970 with an annual payroll of $1.3 billion.[15]

In summary, as can be seen from the material discussed in this section, public transportation can have a significant impact on employment. The contribution which a conveniently available, inexpensive public transit system can make toward linking labor with sources of employment has both direct and indirect benefits. Increased access to job opportunities augments income available to spend in the community for services and retail goods, thereby indirectly stimulating the services and retail, wholesale, and manufacturing employment. Moreover, better transportation for shoppers can be a most effective means of stimulation and revitalization of downtown retail districts, which in many cities across the country have been experiencing declines due to increased automobile use and the development of suburban shopping centers.

Another area in which public transit has a major impact on employment is that of job opportunities created during the development, construction, and operational phases of the transit system. For example, more than 5,000 jobs were generated by the construction of BART in San Francisco, and the Metropolitan Transport Authority of New York provides more than 53,000 jobs associated with administering, operating, and maintaining its system.

Impact on Land-Use Planning and Real Estate Development

General

The introduction and presence of a rapid transit system dramatically affects land-use patterns in metropolitan areas, as evidenced by both historical pattern and future projection. These impacts are highly beneficial and focus on the development of housing, office and commercial centers, appreciation of property values, greater utilization of land and facilities in the CBD, and increased availability of land.

Land Development

The introduction of a rapid transit system has stimulated real estate development such as high-rise apartment developments, office building construction, retail centers, and satellite towns. In Toronto, during the 10-year period from 1952 to 1962, 50 percent of the high-rise apartment construction projects were located on the new subway line.[16] Of the 5,000 apartments currently being added to the housing stock in Toronto, approximately 60 percent are within walking distance of the subway.[17]

A similar positive force has occurred in the office building construction area, where the interaction between rapid transit systems and new construction has produced enormous activity. More than 90 percent (5.1 million square feet) of all office construction in Toronto during the years 1952 to 1962 took place along the rapid transit corridor,[18] with another $2 billion in building construction currently planned or under way.[19] An examination of the development impact of BART confirms the Toronto experience. Since BART was approved by the voters in 1962, more than 500 floors of office space have been added to the San Francisco skyline on Market Street.[20] Further, between 1962 and 1969 office space available or under construction in San Francisco rose from 16,980,000 square feet to 30,345,000 square feet, an increase of 78 percent. All of these new buildings are within five minutes of a BART station. Total construction completed or programmed as of 1969 amounted to $800,000,000 worth of office and civic/recreational facilities.

The effect of BART on the retail district has indeed been startling. In a period when most CBDs have lost retail sales (absolutely and as a percentage of total market), the San Francisco retail district has reversed the decline and increased dollar sales and retained its share of the market. Macy's has constructed an eight-floor, $2.5 million addition; Saks Fifth Avenue has purchased a site on Union Square; and Roos/Atkins has opened a new nine-floor $8.5 million building. The board chairman of Roos/Atkins said, "With the construction of BART, Market Street has become the finest retail street in this country. It influenced our decision to locate here where we can connect directly into the Powell Street station."[21]

Additional expansion of retail activity within the Powell Street station area is highlighted by new shops such as Tiffany, Dunhill, Mark Cross, Peck & Peck, F.A.O. Schwarz, Brentano's, and Doubleday (for additional information on the BART System, see the first section of Chapter 4.

Another approach in using a rapid transit system to shape development is illustrated by the example of the city of Stockholm. There the response to increasing densities and congestion in the central city was to decentralize and use the rapid transit system to establish satellite towns linked to the downtown area. There are presently 18 satellite towns housing from 10,000 to 50,000 people. By the planned introduction of rapid transit links, the metropolitan area of Stockholm has managed to more than double its size without many of the problems of rapid growth.[22]

In both Toronto and Cleveland, significant hubs of activity concentrate at the terminal points of the rapid transit systems. Studies in Cleveland showed rapid transit patrons to live within an area of approximately 15 square miles of the two western end stations (one-half mile apart). The size of such development areas tends to increase with the length of the line and the size of its speed advantage over automobile travel.[23]

Appreciation of Property

An increase in property values per se may only be a private gain to real estate speculators. However, when this value increase is translated into development, then increased assessment, and finally greater primary tax revenue and the secondary employment and income generation, the public benefit becomes obvious. As an example, the Yonge Street subway opened in Toronto in 1954 at an initial total system cost of $67 million. One observer noted:

This small investment in a subway system ignited a $10 billion development explosion along the route from Front and York Streets to the northern terminal, Eglinton Avenue. The appraised value of all the land and facilities in metropolitan Toronto is now $50 billion. An appreciation or $15 billion in physical value has been added in the last 10 years; and of this, two-thirds is attributable to the existence of the Yonge Street subway. Properties along the subway route doubled and tripled, sometimes increasing as much as ten times their original value. Land sales at $125 to $150 per square foot near the downtown stations became common. Between 1952 and 1962, the increase in tax assessment in districts contiguous to the Yonge Street subway line was 45 percent in the downtown area and 107 percent from College Street to Eglinton Avenue. The assessment increase for the rest of the city during the same period averaged 25 percent. On this basis, the Yonge Subway has earned enough new tax dollars to pay its annual amortization costs.[24]

The Toronto experience is confirmed by evidence garnered from earlier studies in New York City of assessed values (and, therefore, tax yields) of land in close proximity to rapid transit station sites before and after the introduction of service. Figure 3-1 illustrates the relationship of cost per square foot and

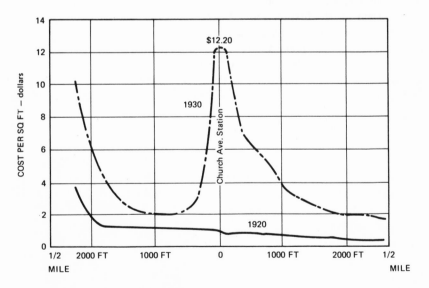

Figure 3-1. Brooklyn Property Value Appreciation. Assessed valuations/ sq ft at distances perpendicular to the Flatbush Ave. Line (Church Ave. Station)[1]. Source: Edward M. Law, "Real Estate and Population Growth along Rapid Transit Lines in the City of New York," *The Municipal Engineers Journal*, Vol. 21, 1935.

proximity to a rapid transit station as experienced in Brooklyn, New York. Not only were values 10 to 12 times higher after the introduction of the station, but they declined consistently with distance from the station. A similar situation occurred as a result of the Cleveland rapid transit system construction.[25]

Land Utilization

The automobile and its supporting system of garage space consumes a large amount of land in the CBD. In some cities the percentage of downtown surface devoted to the moving and storing of automobiles is as high as 65 percent.[26] This wasteful allocation of our resources involves a significant cost. In one projection, it was concluded that if a transit system was not in operation, the CBD would require 6,000 additional parking spaces using from 1,800,000 to 2,400,000 square feet at a cost which would range from $12 million to $56 million.

Another example of the impact of parking showed that "... if a building with 100,000 square feet were built on a 10,000 square foot lot and contained 500 employees, half of whom came by automobile, it would require five levels of parking to handle the need. Hardly feasible."[27] Further, in Miami, planners estimate that in the absence of rapid transit usage, there will be a requirement in the CBD for 3,000,000 square feet of parking space, enough for 10,000 cars. Assuming this need can be met only by garage facilities, costs of providing such storage could reach $30,000,000,[28] and would demand a serious absorption of space otherwise available for an activity of higher economic use.

Possible savings in federal employee parking construction costs by 1990 due to a rapid transit service in Washington, D.C., has been projected to amount to $160,593,100.[29] It was assumed that federal policy would involve provision for 50 percent of indicated demand without transit and 30 percent with transit, and that no additional land would have to be purchased with or without transit. With the reduction in parking construction, the benefits from conservation of federally owned land for economically higher uses would amount to $125,262,600 by 1990.

Costliness of parking lots is illustrated currently in Toronto where a parked car occupies $30,000 to $40,000 worth of land.[30] This land could be developed as a building site and would provide much greater tax revenues. A rapid transit system would lessen this heavy land requirement for parking use. In Los Angeles County, without rapid transit, a local ordinance requires that parking space be provided for employees and customers. The amount of space varies according to the type of establishment but is quite significant. For example, banks must have 1.31 square feet of parking space for every square foot of gross floor space. Table 3-2 presents a full range of requirements.

The presence of rapid transit has created a market for air rights, such as the

Table 3-2
Minimum Parking Space Requirements for Los Angeles

Type of Establishment	Ratio of Parking Space to Gross Floor Space
Banks	1.31
Libraries	1.00
Medical buildings	.92
City-county offices	.88
Post offices	.83
Drug stores	.70
Department stores	.68
Restaurants	.51
YMCA-YWCA	.39
Offices	.36
Variety stores	.27

Source: Stanford Research Institute.

99-year lease of the air rights over the Windemere rapid transit station in the eastern Cleveland suburbs.[31] Similarly, in the East San Francisco Bay area the neighboring cities of El Cerrito and Albany agreed to join with BART in developing a Rapid Transit Parkway along BART's aerial right of way.

Availability

Under certain conditions, without rapid transit, space becomes totally unavailable for automobile requirements. In Miami Beach, planners project 142,000 cars per day will move through the South Beach area by 1985, creating a requirement for two times the currently available surface street lanes. This need exceeds the width of the beach.[32]

By contrast, space can become available through rapid transit as a result of changed land-use patterns. Less space is absorbed for parking, and aerial rights can create additional space. In addition, higher potential population densities can result with rapid transit which permits the choice of allocating space to open areas instead of permitting the potential to be fully placed in residential and commercial uses. This effect has been studied in both Los Angeles and Toronto. The Los Angeles City Planning Commission examined several alternative land-use plans and concluded that with rapid transit, less space is needed for homes, work, and shopping.[33] For a reasonable level of living, only 78 percent of the available land was required with rapid transit, compared to 87 percent without it.

In Toronto, land-use studies showed that land with extensive access to rapid transit could potentially accommodate 10 percent greater population density.[34] This capacity results from clustered high-rise buildings concentrated along the transit corridors. A choice is thus created between actually permitting the higher density or obtaining open-space areas from the available potential.

A significant benefit of rapid transit is its ability to move great numbers of people with minimum utilization of the rapidly dwindling supply of urban land. This is principally due to unique opportunities of building rapid transit lines on median strips of existing freeways, old railroad rights-of-way leading into the CBD, and underneath city streets. A modern rapid transit double-track elevated structure built on "T" supports requires less than 28 feet of right-of-way. In downtown Chicago and in San Francisco, rapid transit now occupies the center space over existing downtown freeways. In addition, a new six-mile stretch of rapid transit in Boston, built on the existing right-of-way of the New Haven Railroad, is expected to carry 35,000 passengers per day by 1975, at virtually no cost to the existing supply of land. If the same people commuted by highway, it would require six to eight lanes of new paved surface and cause a heavy absorption of CBD land.

Urban arterial highways require, by Federal Highway Administration standards, a minimum width of 11 feet per land and eight feet per shoulder. In many cases, however, cities will have more stringent local standards requiring much more width for shoulders and median strips. A six-lane urban freeway consequently may require widths from 90 to 150 feet for the right-of-way, depending on the local highway standards and practices. For each mile of urban freeway, 11 to 34 acres of relatively scarce urban land must be acquired, and this requirement does not include space for new feeder lanes or additional downtown parking. Not only does rapid transit absorb potentially much less urban land than a highway required to move similar numbers of people, but it also does not directly escalate the price of urban land by diminishing the land supply, as may occur for highway construction. One estimate for San Jose's CBD placed the carrying capacity of a two-track rail rapid transit system with six-car trains at 12,000 to 43,000 persons per hour per track. Automobiles can carry 750 to 4,000 per highway or street lane (or if filled to capacity, as many as 12,000 persons) per hour.[35] However, lanes required to move equivalent passengers by automobile would be 10 times as great, without even considering the space needed for automobile storage or the possible environmental impact.

Summary

Rapid transit systems have stimulated important real estate development, property value appreciation, and improved land utilization and availability. In Toronto, several billion dollars of high-rise apartment and office building construction has produced enormous growth along the transit corridors. San

Francisco has recently experienced a dramatic reversal of the decline in its Market Street retail district with office building, retail, and civic facility construction approaching $1 billion. In both San Francisco and Cleveland, suburban development has spurted in the regions extending outward from rapid transit terminals. This type of activity has focused in Stockholm, Sweden, through the development of satellite towns containing clustered populations of 10,000 to 50,000.

With the development of land made attractive through rapid transit installations, such cities as Toronto have experienced strongly rising property values, higher assessed values, tax revenues, and ultimately public benefits through secondary employment and income creation. The strength of rapid transit's impact on property values was measured for New York City as well, where values were positively and strikingly correlated with proximity to transit stops.

Rapid transit permits more efficient land utilization by relieving CBDs of the need to provide space for movement and off-street storage of automobiles. Estimates of the savings possible in this area for federal employees in Washington, D.C., totaled $286 million, when rapid transit becomes available. In addition, air rights over transit rights-of-way can be developed over freeways.

Land availability is enhanced by rapid transit. Both in Toronto and Los Angeles, high-rise apartment construction along transit routes has increased potential population densities and generated the option of allocating more land to open spaces. Further, to the extent rapid transit can substitute for automobile usage, land otherwise needed for additional freeways or streets is retained for other preferred uses. This is particularly important to Miami Beach, which simply does not contain sufficient total land to accommodate the projected increase in automobile traffic by 1985. Moreover, the quantity of land absorbed for a transit right-of-way is one-third to one-fifth that needed for an urban freeway, excluding freeway needs for feeder lanes or off-street downtown parking. Under certain conditions in which rapid transit can be built over old unused rail rights-of-way, freeway median strips or underground urban land absorption is eliminated almost entirely.

Impact on the Environment

Air Pollution

Within the urban environment there are numerous human and physical elements which interact to create what is rapidly becoming one of the most critical problems within our cities, the problem of air pollution. It has been well established that one of the primary causes of air pollution throughout the country is the automobile. The car's internal combustion engine generates a very high percentage (in terms of weight) of the total air pollutants emitted.

Table 3-3 presents 1968 estimates on emissions from motor vehicles, as reported by the U.S. Environmental Protection Agency. These figures show that one-half of the hydrocarbons, one-third of the oxides of nitrogen, two-thirds of the carbon monoxide, and nine-tenths of the lead-bearing particulate emissions in the air are caused by exhaust and evaporation from motor vehicles. As the result of further findings reported in July 1970, it has been calculated that approximately one-sixth pound of nitrogen oxide, one-half pound of hydrocarbon, and 3.1 pounds of carbon monoxide are emitted for every gallon of gasoline consumed by internal combustion engines. Of the five major pollutants of our atmosphere—carbon monoxide, hydrocarbons, nitrogen oxide, particulates, and sulfur dioxide—only the latter two are emitted from industrial and other stationary sources in greater quantities than can be attributed to mobile sources.[36]

Although the influence of air pollution on human health is not completely understood, there is evidence that it is an important factor in chronic respiratory diseases and in susceptibility to upper respiratory infections.[37] According to the Los Angeles Public Health Service, carbon monoxide produces headaches, loss of visual acuity, and decreased muscular coordination. Hydrocarbons have produced cancer in laboratory animals and play a major role in the formation of photochemical smog which damages crops and trees and reacts with materials resulting in the deterioration of rubber textiles and dyes.[38]

As disturbing as is the picture drawn by the preceding statements and figures, the air pollution problem is more than compounded by the locational incidence of emissions. Air pollution is a critical problem in our cities for two reasons: (i) it is in urban areas that the overwhelming proportion of automobile travel is concentrated; and (ii) most carbon monoxide is released during acceleration, hence intermittent driving in stop-and-go city traffic results in a significantly greater release of pollutants than uncongested steady driving.[39]

Table 3-4 which gives figures on commuter exposure to carbon monoxide for

Table 3-3
Estimated Emissions from Motor Vehicles

Pollutant	Proportion of Total Emissions (All Sources)	Potential Emissions Without Controls (Million Tons)		Emissions With Controls (Million Tons)	
		1968	1975	1968	1975
Hydrocarbon	1/2	20	30	18.4	10.5
Carbon Monoxide	2/3	130	155	94	72
Nitrogen Oxides	1/3	7.3	8.2	7.3	7.2
Lead-Bearing Particulates	9/10	0.35	0.42	0.35	0.04

Source: Research Triangle Institute, using data from the U.S. Environmental Protection Agency.

various cities provides some indication of the severity of that one type of air pollution in major urban areas. California has established 30 parts per million (ppm) for eight-hours exposure and 120 ppm for one-hour exposure to carbon monoxide as a health and safety level standard. Table 3-4 shows that in many cities commuters are exposed to carbon monoxide levels well above the standard.

Air pollution is one of the social costs associated with private automobile transportation. Since individual drivers are not assessed for the cost or disutility of this pollution, social costs diverge from private costs. There have been several attempts to estimate the costs to society of such an externality. One approach has been to compare the direct out-of-pocket costs of living among areas with different levels of air pollution. Expenditures on house-painting costs, car-wash outlays, curtain-cleaning expenses, shampoo purchases, and general housecleaning expenses were some of the variables examined. A 1967 study of Greater Washington, D.C., calculated that air pollution costs a family living in the central city $335 more per year than a similar family living outside the metropolitan area.[40]

Another approach has been to estimate the effects of air pollution on property values on the assumption that, ceteris paribus, the additional costs (both tangible and intangible) associated with living in an area with high levels of pollution would be reflected in lower real estate prices. A 1960 study of the St. Louis metropolitan area arrived at an estimate of a $245 decline in property values per house with each 0.25 mg. rise in sulphur trioxide levels, as an index of air pollution.[41]

The emissions of unburned hydrocarbons, nitrate oxides, carbon monoxide, lead particles, rubber dust, and other substances must be contrasted with the virtually pollution-free operation of electrically powered rapid transit cars. Although some experts assert that any reduction in air pollution has immeasurable value, the actual economic value relative to the public's health and property is unknown. Nevertheless, in the cost-benefit analysis of the five-corridor rapid transit system prepared for the Southern California Rapid Transit District, Stanford Research Institute (SRI) attempted to identify the quantifiable aspects of the reduction of pollution resulting from the diversion of commuters from automobile to rapid transit. Based upon projections of a diversion equivalent to 4,600,000 vehicle-miles to the proposed five-corridor rapid transit system, it was estimated that emissions would be decreased by 231 tons per day. It was further calculated that reductions in stop-and-go traffic and increases in slow speeds during rush hours would result in an additional decrease of 69 tons per day.[42]

The SRI study of the Los Angeles area also calculated savings due to a reduction in need for diverted commuters to make expenditures on automobile pollution control devices:

The cost per year to the motorist is the $80 for the devices divided by the average lifetime of an automobile (5.8 years), or $13.80. The number of

Table 3-4
Commuter Exposure to Carbon Monoxide—20-30 Min. Runs in Traffic (Concentrations in ppm)

City	Year	Route Type	No. Runs	Exposure During Run			Brief Peak Exposure		
				Min.	Avg.	Max.	Min.	Avg.	Max.
Atlanta	1966	Expressway	10	12	23	35	50	73	92
		Arterial	9	21	30	40	37	62	91
		Center City	7	13	21	27	33	49	75
Baltimore	1966	Expressway	18	2	9	21	6	32	79
		Arterial	25	6	17	33	14	37	82
		Center City	14	15	24	38	28	54	92
Chicago	1966	Expressway	34	13	24	37	24	52	91
	1967	Expressway	34	3	20	35	7	43	86
	1966	Arterial	51	7	16	31	16	32	59
	1967	Arterial	29	1	16	41	3	32	68
	1966	Center City	17	24	32	55	36	58	91
	1967	Center City	10	19	34	53	45	70	109
Cincinnati	1966	Expressway	7	3	10	15	8	22	32
	1967	Expressway	24	7	15	34	12	27	53
	1966	Arterial	25	3	17	32	6	36	79
	1967	Arterial	11	9	15	19	18	32	50
	1966	Center City	8	17	29	50	30	56	96
	1967	Center City	6	12	20	32	19	36	71
Denver	1966	Expressway	24	10	21	38	20	40	71
		Arterial	41	16	32	61	35	65	138
		Center City	10	21	34	54	36	69	96
Detroit	1966	Expressway	48	11	25	54	22	51	116
		Arterial	51	14	25	41	34	54	91
		Center City	16	15	25	36	33	51	85
Houston	1966	Expressway	31	2	16	39	9	29	74
		Arterial	23	5	15	33	13	36	82
		Center City	14	16	38	70	32	75	98

City	Year	Type							
Los Angeles	1966	Expressway	87	9	29	62	23	52	102
		Arterial	15	24	38	60	45	74	147
		Center City	17	27	40	60	44	68	111
Louisville	1966	Expressway	14	2	8	21	6	17	30
		Arterial	14	4	16	31	8	32	61
		Center City	10	16	23	33	28	40	62
Minneapolis-St. Paul	1966 (M.)	Arterial	59	10	23	41	18	52	130
	(St. P)	Center City	15	20	30	45	35	52	>91
		Center City	13	21	35	65	28	56	>91
New York	1966	Expressway	31	8	23	44	15	47	91
	1967	Expressway	17	5	21	39	16	45	141
	1966	Center City	47	14	32	58	24	57	91
	1967	Center City	30	9	27	42	16	50	119
Philadelphia	1967	Expressway	20	8	17	38	17	38	94
		Arterial	40	9	22	38	17	40	82
		Center City	20	18	29	38	37	55	80
Phoenix	1966	Expressway	39	12	23	50	18	40	83
		Arterial	26	13	27	43	26	56	87
		Center City	12	27	38	54	44	72	105
St. Louis	1967	Expressway	37	2	10	22	7	22	57
		Arterial	38	8	17	34	17	36	70
		Center City	19	15	28	50	28	56	109
Washington	1967	Expressway	35	2	12	33	5	27	76
		Arterial	17	10	20	30	22	40	86
		Center City	34	8	26	63	13	45	116

Source: National Air Sampling Network, NCAPC, as cited in Kamrass, et al., *Concepts for Evaluating Center City Transportation Programs and Projects*, p. 39.

automobiles projected for 1980 is 4,231,859, so that in 1980, it will cost $58,399,634 to control 8,030 million pounds of pollutants, or $.00725 per pound of reduction or $14.50 per ton. The 300-ton reduction, therefore, amounts to $4,350 per day or a benefit of $1,587,750 per year.[43]

Another study has focused on the effect on air pollution levels of diverting commuters from automobiles to bus transit. In this study it was estimated that if the transit system were not available, the additional pollutants per year for the Sacramento area, excluding weekend traffic would be approximately 1,007 tons of carbon monoxide, 240 tons of hydrocarbons, and 37 tons of oxides of nitrogen. These estimates assumed an area average of 1.36 persons per automobile and a 20 percent reduction in travel by captive riders caused by the lack of transportation facilities.[44]

Noise

It has only been within relatively recent years that open expression has been given to the concept of noise as a prime element of urban pollution. Illustrative of the magnitude of the problem is the statement by some authorities that New York citizens start to show a hearing loss at 25, contrasted with primitive tribes who do not show one until 70. Scientists predict that if city noise continues to rise at its present rate of one decibel a year, urban residents could be stone, or at least tone, deaf by the year 2000. The Surgeon General estimates that between six and 16 million Americans are exposed to possible hearing damage from occupational noise.[45]

To date few noise level standards have been applied to ground transportation, although standards have been established for a variety of applications, including aircraft and factories. As a general reference guide, Figure 3-2 shows the sound pressure levels (SPL) produced by a variety of sources.[46] By itself, however, SPL does not indicate the human response to noise, because annoyance varies with the frequency or pitch of the noise as well as with the intensity. For example, the maximum constant background noise for factories, set by the Department of Labor, is 90 decibels, which is also the decibel of train whistles. Yet, to the human ear, the higher frequency train whistle is more annoying than lower frequency factory noise at the same intensity.

Although the noise levels generated by most subway systems are relatively high, the tunnels serve to contain the noise, making it more an internal annoyance to riders than a contributing factor to external urban environmental pollution. This, of course, is not the case for surface rail lines.

New transit equipment has been designed to reduce noise to a minimum, and in this respect has far exceeded the progress being made in the production of new automobiles. An experimental steam-powered bus being used in the

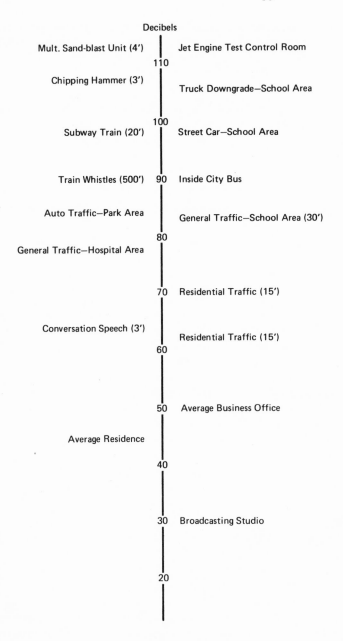

Figure 3-2. Selected Sound Levels. Source: M. Kamrass, J. Crane, P. Hughes, and E. Parker, *Concepts for Evaluating Center City Transportation Programs and Projects*, Urban Mass. Transportation Project, December 1969, p. 39.

Alameda Contra Costa Transit District, for example, is reported to be substantially quieter than the standard diesel bus engine. The BART system is being designed to have very low decibel levels also (see Part II).

Quantifying the potential impact of rapid rail systems in reducing the amount of urban noise is not really possible given the current state of the art for acoustical engineering. As explained by members of Stanford Research Institute:

Rapid transit should have little effect on overall transportation noise. Some auto traffic will be diverted, but freeways, even when free flowing, will still be as noisy as before . . . No apparent credit can be identified in noise reduction. A mere "plus" is taken as the total annual benefit.[47]

Summary

The problem of air pollution and, to a somewhat lesser extent, noise nuisances in our urban environment have become two of the most urgent issues confronting major U.S. cities today. The information presented in this section clearly illustrates the staggering amount of air pollution caused by automobiles. The figures projected by the U.S. Environmental Protection Agency for auto emissions by the year 1975 show an expected generation of 180 billion pounds of pollutants. This is equivalent to the release of 890 pounds for every person in the United States. The exact long-range consequences of the effect of foul air on the public's health and in the magnitude of its impact on property values has yet to be fully determined. Moreover, scientific findings, cited in the preceding pages, have pointed to the danger of loss of hearing and reduction in general physical and psychological well-being of urban dwellers who are constantly exposed to excessive noise levels.

Certainly air pollution and noise reduction should constitute a major objective of any transportation program. Diversion of motorists to public transit would result in a sizable reduction in air pollutants emitted and traffic noise generated, due to both a decrease in the total number of pollution sources and to better traffic flow, which, in turn, permits more efficient combustion in the car's engine and less horn-honking from stop-and-go driving conditions.

Part II
Case Studies of Urban
Transit Systems

Introduction

In Part I, the individual objectives of overall transportation policy were discussed in terms of the contribution of public transit toward meeting those objectives. In Part II, we will examine on a program-by-program basis the impact of each program on attaining the objectives. The programs are divided into three major categories: rapid rail, bus transit, and commuter rail. Five rapid rail systems, five subcategories of bus transit capital investments, and two commuter rail programs are presented.

Quantitative results of operating evidence or projections related to particular impacts have been included, whenever possible. When statistical information was not available for a specific impact, it is not explicitly discussed; however, this is not to imply that the impact does not exist as a result of the transit system under discussion.

Our purpose in analyzing these programs was to develop additional information on the objectives of public transit in meeting broad urban goals. In the process of research for Part II, we identified several other objectives of public transit which were then added to the original list.

The discussion of each system first establishes the need for an alternative to the auto/highway mode within a particular geographic area, and then focuses on benefits to users, operators, and the community. At the end of each program discussion, we have summarized the economic and social impacts of that specific program.

4 Rapid Rail Transit

San Francisco Bay Area Rapid Transit (BART) System

General

BART, as originally proposed, was to be a new rapid transit system covering 103 miles in the San Francisco-Oakland Bay area. When completed it will have cost over $1.4 billion to construct and be made operational. Begun in 1965, the construction period originally was estimated to be eight and one half years. As of January 1972, the system was 77 percent complete and was expected to be operational by March 1972, although the entire 103-mile system is not now expected to be completed until 1980.[1] The system will be paid for by (i) a .05 percent levy on all assessable properties in the district which includes Alameda, Contra Costa, Marin, San Francisco, and San Mateo Counties, (ii) a general obligation bond issue, (iii) operating revenues, and (iv) the California Toll Bridge Authority.[2]

The system itself is a state-of-the-art concept and the first regional network as such. With a top speed of 80 mph, the rapid transit rail cars will operate with 450 amp., 1,000 volt, 60 cycle power, on completely grade-separated rights of way at 90-second peak hour headways. Further, the system will be controlled automatically by a computer.[3] Plans also include automation of fare collection, whereby regular patrons will be issued charge cards to be inserted in identification devices.[4] Fares will range from 3.2 cents per mile to 2.25 cents per mile, with an additional 10 cents for each trip through the Bay Tunnel.

Need for Rapid Transit in the Bay Area

Certain characteristics of metropolitan development make the San Francisco Bay area highly dependent on effective transportation.

1. The area is large and growing. Its 1960 population figure of 2,648,800 represented an 88 percent increase in 20 years, and the population of the entire nine-county area is forecast to reach 8,000,000 persons by the year 2000. Further, the bay and the surrounding mountains that dominate the areas topography have resulted in a settlement pattern of the population concentrated along the shores of the bay and the nearby valleys. This condition forces a great

many people to rely on transportation along a limited number of overburdened central arteries.

2. Residential population has exhibited a decentralizing trend in recent years. Studies indicate that without transit, decentralization eventually would weaken the CBD's economic base and cost the bay area almost 200,000 jobs. A good example of the effects of the decentralization of population is Oakland, where the population fell by 10 percent between 1950 and 1960. It has been estimated that, due to this decline in population, Oakland lost over $100 million in annual purchasing power, which led to a lower real estate tax base, thus pushing downtown Oakland into a state of economic decline.[5]

3. Estimates in 1960 showed that commuter traffic over the bay crossings was increasing faster than the population; peak-hour traffic across the Bay and Golden Gate Bridges represented over 50 percent of total daily traffic and was rapidly accelerating. It was further estimated that by 1975, ten new lanes of traffic would have to be added to the Oakland-San Francisco crossing alone, just to service rush-hour traffic. Engineers determined that by then-current highway standards the bay crossings were already inadequate to handle the traffic volume at that time.

4. Intracounty commuter trips were projected to grow by almost 45 percent from 1960 to 1975. About 75 percent of all commuter trips are presently into downtown San Francisco.

5. Sociologists also point out that, along with the burgeoning regional population patterns, there are ever widening geographical distances among races which will eventually mean wider psychological and social separation. For example, the U.S. Department of Commerce Census figures for 1965 indicated that the San Francisco-Oakland metropolitan area, where most of the bay area ghettoes exist, experienced only a 4.8 percent increase in employment between 1951 and 1965, while employment in the suburban ring rose 95.2 percent over the same period. It is hoped that the new regional transit will help to ameliorate this growing problem by providing reverse commuting opportunities to those still living in the urban core.[6]

Benefits of the BART System

A summary of the projected impact of the BART system, expressed in monetary terms, is shown in Table 4-1.

1. *User benefits:*

Time savings. In economic feasibility studies conducted for both the alternative four- and five-county systems, time savings were assessed as having the greatest potential value. The computations used to derive the time-savings figure shown in Table 4-1 were based on estimated time savings per passenger of 15 minutes twice a day for 250 working days per year, and time saved was valued at 1.52¢ per minute or 92¢ per hour.

Table 4-1

Economic Benefits Summary, Estimated Measurable Benefits and Costs in 1975, Bay Area Rapid Transit System

	Five-County System	Four-County System
Time Savings		
Person trips	$30,526,000	$26,400,000
Motor freight movement	2,875,000	2,500,000
Reductions in costs from diversion of traffic to rapid transit		
Accidents	1,172,000	1,000,000
Insurance premiums	2,104,000	1,800,000
Automobile operation	27,785,000	24,100,000
Parking charges	6,295,000	5,500,000
Bridge tolls	2,846,000	2,100,000
Traffic control	457,000	400,000
Present transit systems	19,270,000	15,800,000
Total savings in time and expenses	$93,330,000	$79,600,000
Deduct rapid transit fares	51,150,000	39,900,000
Net measurable transportation benefits in 1975	$42,180,000	$39,700,000
All values expressed in 1960 dollars.		

Source: EBASCO Service, Inc.

Improved comfort and safety. Benefits of comfort and safety for passengers are being incorporated at all levels of testing and development of new equipment for the BART system. For example, sound measurements were taken to determine interior noise and typical underfloor noise levels of the test cars. In addition, data were obtained on the Pennsylvania Railroad to provide information on the noise level inside multiple-unit cars when traveling in tunnels and outdoors. The test results and observations indicated that wheel damping is an effective means of reducing wheel squeal and that the wayside noise reduction produced by wheel damping occurs most significantly for frequencies higher than 500 cps, which is the portion of the frequency spectrum that contributes most strongly to annoyance.[7]

All specifications for supplier contracts devote particular attention to the design of quiet equipment. Limitations on noise levels include the following:

a. Traction motors and bearing sets shall not produce noise levels greater than 85 dba, 15 ft. from the center of the track with wheels spinning under no-load conditions at all speeds from zero to 60 mph equivalent car speed.

b. Undercar components and operating systems, except traction motors and gearing shall not produce noise levels greater than 65 dba each 15 ft. from the center of the noise producing equipment while the equipment is operating at normal conditions with the car at rest.

c. The car body floor structure in its complete form, including all noise leakage at locations such as openings in the car for air supply and return ducts, shall have an average transmission loss of at least 35 dba in the octave band with 1,000 Hz center frequency.

d. The car body walls, windows, roof and doors shall have an average transmission loss of at least 30 dba in the octave band with 1,000 Hz center frequency.

e. Car interior noise level. With the air refrigeration and distribution system, the motor alternator, and the air compressor (or hydraulic power unit) operating normally, noise in the interior of the car shall exceed neither 78 dbc nor 65 dba at all points at least 1 ft. from any surface. With any one of these units operating normally, car interior noise, measured similarly, shall exceed neither 75 dbc nor 60 dba.

f. Door operation noise. Noise produced by operation of the car doors only shall exceed neither 80 dbc nor 70 dba anywhere in the car except within 1 ft. of the doors or door pockets.[8]

Another example of user benefits in this area is the development of improved braking systems. A fundamental safety requirement for the Bay Area Rapid Transit system is the ability to stop a train consistently within a prescribed distance under the most adverse set of conditions. For the vehicle specifications, a braking system utilizing self-ventilated disc and caliper on each axle was specified. Composition linings will be used. The disc type brake displays less variations of tractive effort with environmental changes and braking history than the tread type, and is preferred from that point of view. It is expected to be quieter in operation than the tread type. A hydraulically actuated braking system has been selected for the BART transit vehicles.[9]

Savings in automobile ownership and operating costs. It is anticipated that the BART system will virtually eliminate student dependence on automobiles, because with few exceptions, bay area colleges are either near rapid transit stations or close to feeder bus lines. Within a few hundred feet of BART stations, for example, are Laney College with 7,000 students, City College of San Francisco with 12,000 students, and the University of California at Berkeley with 27,000 students. It should be noted that Laney College and City College of San Francisco are particularly important to the economic and social welfare of underprivileged people. Both institutions offer one- and two-year occupational and vocational training, as well as academic studies which parallel four-year college offerings. Both are local institutions run by local people, and therefore can respond with more flexibility to the local needs of the poor. In addition, hundreds of part-time and night students attend small downtown private schools for special instruction in medical, dental, electronic, clerical, accounting, secretarial, and other occupational specialties; these facilities also will be well served by the BART regional transit system.

Of primary importance to the penny-pinching college students is the elimination of automobile expenses which have been estimated by recent federal and AAA surveys to run between 11 and 13.6 cents per mile. In the bay area it costs a car owner between $4.40 and $5.40 for a 20-mile, two-way commutation every day. Even a 10-mile home-to-campus commutation, then, can be financially devastating to the average college student, much more to the underprivileged one.[10]

2. *Operator benefits.* Lower operating costs and increased efficiency will be the prime benefits resulting from the automatic train control functions to be utilized by BART.[a] Automated functions will include dispatch of trains into revenue service, assignment of train identification numbers, assignment of train routes, monitoring and control of train departures from stations and their headways, removal of trains from revenue service, signal-operating discrepancies, initiation of remedial actions, log system operation, and display of operating status.[11]

The BART automatic fare collection system also will save in operating costs, due to the reduction of personnel required for traditional manual methods of fare collection.

3. *Community benefits*

Land-use planning and real estate development. An effect of the development of the new BART system which is difficult to quantify, but which already has a high degree of visible impact, is the stimulus to real estate development. One need only look at pictures of Market Street, an area that a few years ago had a dilapidated, rundown appearance and was only of marginal commercial value. Today new construction is everywhere in evidence—$1 billion in new construction over the past five years. In all, over 400 stories of new office space in the vicinity of Market Street are planned, under construction, or now leasing and operating. Included in this is the mammoth $250-million Embarcadero Center. Along Market Street, subway stations are literally being extended into skyscrapers by means of private access entrances 25 feet beneath the sidewalks.[12]

Oakland also is expected to experience an increase of 4.3 million square feet of office space demand over the next 20 years. As the developers have commented, "No one will admit that the commercial development was caused by the new BART line that runs down Market Street. All anybody will say is that the development wouldn't be there without it." In short, the BART system has opened the door to new urban development.

BART has also opened the door to suburban development in places like Walnut Creek. Dillingham Corp. now is putting up two 10-story office buildings, heretofore unfeasible because of the relative inaccessibility of Walnut Creek from other key commercial centers in the bay area. In Pittsburg, California, a full 20-minute drive from the nearest transit stop, Kaufman & Broad is working

---

[a]Automatic train control for BART was necessitated by the 90-second headway, high-speed, and long-train aspects of the system.

on a $95 million residential development as well as $65 million in other housing in nearby towns. Therefore, Pittsburg now offers the public a viable location to live, which was not true before the existence of BART. Furthermore, the developers can build and sell a house for $20,000, a more popular price, because land is now cheaper in the outlying areas. Here, again, BART was the catalyst. In this way both the public and the developers benefit by the new supply of land, while in places like Walnut Creek, real estate is reaching all time high values because of the commercial attractiveness. This situation will, in turn, create a better tax base and stimulate the region's economic growth.[13]

Another real estate benefit—largely to existing home owners in suburban communities—resulting from the installation of rapid transit stations is the increase in property values. Studies in the bay area indicate that residential properties of similar kinds increase in value by approximately $1,500 for every ten minutes' less of travel time to the major employment centers.[14]

In planning for longer term regional growth, it is anticipated that the new transit will provide a means of reversing the economic state of decline experienced in the East Bay areas around Oakland due to the past decentralization of population.

Reduced congestion. It has been estimated that the BART system will carry 40 percent of all rush-hour traffic, with a correspondingly great impact in reducing highway congestion.

Increased employment. The BART system has already had a great effect on the employment picture within the bay area. The $1.4 billion project, expended through a local contract, has involved a payroll of up to 5,000 construction workers with a minority makeup of 33 to 35 percent.[15]

With regard to further employment opportunities, as written in *Rapid Transit*:

Initial BART planning, tailored in part by the region's topography, located 16 rapid transit stations in neighborhoods formally classed as "target" poverty areas by local Economic Opportunity Councils. Maps based on information supplied by anti-poverty officials identify these areas. Some of them contain ghetto neighborhoods.

BART stations in or near newly developing employment centers of Southern Alameda County, from San Leandro to Fremont, are within 15 to 30 minutes of the BART station in West Oakland. The Spanish-speaking communities of Southern Alameda County and San Francisco's Mission District are within minutes of both suburban and downtown employment centers.[16]

Summary

The San Francisco Bay Area Rapid Transit (BART) System is due to begin operation in late 1972. User benefits are to include time savings of 15 minutes per trip per day per passenger; comfort and safety equipment design, including minimized noise and improved brake system design; and savings in automobile ownership and operating costs of 11 to 14 cents per mile. Principal operator benefits will accrue through reduced operating costs and increased efficiency resulting from automatic train control functions and automatic fare collection.

The bay area community has already undergone very intensive and extensive new real estate development, both in downtown San Francisco, where $1 billion worth of new construction has occurred along Market Street in five years, and in suburban regions, where numerous commercial and residential developments have now been undertaken, using the suburbs' lower cost land as well as retaining good access to the central city. Other community benefits will include creation of higher property values, accruing to existing home and other property owners; reversal of economic declines in urban East Bay areas which were otherwise becoming isolated as the population became decentralized; significant reductions in peak-hour gateway traffic congestion; increased employment, both in construction of the $1.3 billion BART system and in new construction, industrial, and commercial positions; and finally improved employment opportunities for minority groups, who constituted 33 percent of the BART construction force and who will have better access to the bay area jobs.

Benefits of the BART system which were not discussed in detail above include:

1. Savings in cost to operators through the implementation of the most automated system available, including automatic fare collection.
2. Reduction of air pollution of 300 tons of pollutants daily, as discussed in Part I.
3. Airport access, a significant problem in the bay area, for which a solution has not yet been resolved.
4. Benefits to the aged, the young, and the handicapped, which are thought to be considerable, but for which limited backup data are available.

The Broad Street Subway of Philadelphia

General

In 1971, a study was undertaken to determine the user needs and benefits of an improved Broad and Columbia subway station in connection with the proposed northeast extension of the Broad Street subway.[17] The proposed extension was to run approximately six miles to the northeastern part of the city with the terminus at Rhawn Street. The estimated costs for this extension are $144 million, but it is not clear how the branch will be financed. The extension, as well as the entire Philadelphia subway system, is leased and operated by the Southeastern Pennsylvania Transportation Authority (SEPTA).

Since the new subway station at Broad Street and Columbia Avenue was considered to be an important functional part of the immediate community as well as a gateway to Temple University, a design study was undertaken by the Temple University College of Engineering, sponsored by the Philadelphia City Planning Commission and the U.S. Department of Transportation. The purpose of the study was to analyze the impact subway station design has on local communities and how well-designed stations and station renovations can benefit them. The objective of the study was to produce an optimum station design concept that would integrate the functions of the transit stop with surrounding development.

The redesign of the subway stop was developed in several short- and long-range phases, described briefly as follows:

1. Short-range Phase I improvements include the addition of personal safety features such as a security guard, alarm system, shortened platforms, and improved lighting. Some relocation of turnstiles and basic repairs, including new flooring, would be desirable, but no major structural changes were planned. The total cost was estimated at $200,000.
2. Short-range Phase II station improvements include the addition of straight-run stairs with three landings and at least one escalator. Costs for these structural improvements would be about $300,000.
3. Phase III improvements for the longer range would include additional structural changes, such as skylights, open court links, and a pedestrian bridge to link the north- and south-bound platforms. Costs would be approximately $500,000.
4. A fourth phase of improvements was recommended for the longer range also. These include a covered pedestrian bridge, completion of open courts and mezzanine links, and an automated fare collection system. These improvements would cost $376,000.

Need for the Subway Station Improvements

Needs for the redevelopment of the Broad and Columbia Avenue station were established largely through a consumer preference sampling survey and by a study of the psychological and physical effects of the subway environment. The consumer preference study resulted in the following conclusions regarding needs for station redesign:[b]

1. Safety—minimal improvements in safety to enhance the user's perception of personal as well as actual safety. This would result in increased usage.
2. Beautification—61 percent of the sample said they would use the subway more often if it were merely cleaned and painted. 73 percent expressed a

---

[b]522 individuals were polled.

desire for design features allowing for fresh air, sunlight and a view of the street level.

3. Recreational, cultural, and commercial facilities—61 percent of the sample expressed a need for recreational and cultural facilities near the station; 62 percent would use additional shopping facilities if they were near the station.

A study of psychological and physical effects of the subway environment produced recommendations for the following:

1. Safety—An alarm system and emergency telephone is needed to reduce psychological barriers to using the station, especially during the off-peak hours, and to help others in distress on the station premises. The illumination level should be raised to 100 foot candles to ensure proper illumination of all objects in the station. This would also contribute to perceived safety.

2. Comfort—Sound levels should be reduced to the 80 decibel range to ensure comfortable hearing levels. This would be more conducive to conversation and reduce the disconcerting and annoying factor of interference with speech and listening. Further, the discomfort of crowding at the turnstiles should be eliminated and more effective means of ensuring smooth and unbroken traffic flow should be designed into the station. Finally, a more comfortable seating arrangement is needed to reduce the frequency of riders' intruding into the "intimate space" of one another. (Psychologists define this "intimate space" as 18 inches to the front and sides of the individual.)

3. Beautification—Color must be considered as part of the complex, aesthetic environment. Certain colors are associated with certain moods; for example, blue and green are associated with pleasantness and coolness. Brighter colors are also needed to enhance the reflection of good light.

A design study was then conducted, and based on its findings and the findings of the user survey and psychological studies, some architectural objectives were established as follows:

1. The Broad Street subway serves as a natural link between major institutions in the city, such as three universities, City Hall, a major commercial district, museums, and sports stadiums. All lie directly on the subway line. The station design and environment, therefore, should be reflective of certain ties between institutions.

2. Stations serve as gateways to surrounding communities and in many ways are the focal points. Thus, station design should enhance this functional quality and provide easy and convenient access and passage between the transit and the community.

3. Subway stops, in many cases, must facilitate modal splits in transportation.

4. Subway stations must be safe, pleasant, and efficient in serving transit users. Safety was found to be the most important concern on the part of transit riders.

Benefits of Subway Station Restoration and
Improvements

An analysis of specific benefits to result from various aspects of the redesign of the station at Broad and Columbia are summarized below.

1. *User benefits.* Riders will benefit from fewer accidents in dark areas, less crime, and generally a greater feeling of comfort and security. In 1970, more than 80 crimes were reported in subway stations, and countless more went unreported. In 1969, 121 accidents and incidents were reported, many due to rowdyism, and one-third due to poorly lit stairways. In this case, improved lighting and painting would be of substantial benefit to subway users, in terms of both aesthetic appearances and safety.

Another benefit noticed is shortened platforms to ensure safer station stops and a greater sense of visual awareness of the entire platform area. Philadelphia now has some long, dark platform areas which, because of length and poor lighting, have many blind spots and dark areas.

Graphic aids would benefit users by directing them in an innovative and informative way. It is not purely frivolous that "subway station art" has recently come into vogue. Further, improved exits and entrances would benefit users by providing easier, more convenient, and less congested platform access and circulation. Overall transit is perceived to be greater if there are fewer bottlenecks in platform movement. Additional turnstiles are often needed to provide better access.

Pedestrian "bridging" between platforms benefits the nonuser by giving him a safe way to cross the street, as well as the user by giving him a way to make a "U-turn" in case he misses a stop.

Open courts and skylights have the benefits of allowing sunlight and fresh air into the station, of visually integrating subway platform with surrounding environment, of providing a convenient and attractive transition between subway and adjacent commercial or institutional developments, of adding beautification, and of providing an area of congregation away from the subway platform and turnstiles.

2. *Operator benefits.* Operator benefits of station improvements are largely monetary, measured in terms of increased ridership and reduced costs. The following is an analysis of the incremental benefits of specific improvements as projected for the Broad and Columbia station redevelopment:

a. A security guard system would cost about $42,000 per year for 24-hour guard service plus closed circuit TV equipment and would result in increased ridership. Results of the consumer survey and assumptions concerning the amount of extra ridership due to additional perceived safety were used to calculate the amount—$24,000—of extra annual revenue that would be realized. Also, with one man in a kiosk with a closed circuit TV surveillance, $31,000 of labor savings would result, and a total return of $55,000 in cash benefits would be realized by the security guard proposal. Platform shortening, improved lighting, and repainting would increase ridership, but no measurable benefits were calculated.

b. Improved exits and entrances would result in better, easier, and more convenient circulation and platform access. Overall transit speed is perceived to be faster if there is less of a bottleneck at the turnstiles. Simply rearranging turnstiles and adding three new turnstiles would cost about $22,000 and result in an estimated $5,500 per year increase in ridership and fares.

c. Improved lighting, including an eye-level intensity of 75 foot candles and spot illumination of key functional areas (such as kiosks, turnstiles, graphics, reading areas, stairs and platform edges), will improve visual capability and perceived safety and result in increased ridership. The cost for improved lighting in the Broad and Columbia station was estimated at $26,000, while the fares would increase an estimated $21,000 per year.

d. Pedestrian bridging between platforms was estimated at $180,000, while the increase in ridership was determined to be worth $10,000 per year.

e. Open courts and skylights would cost about $191,000, while increased attractiveness to riders would result in an estimated $21,000 increase in annual fares.

f. Automated fare collection equipment provides the benefits of quicker service and the elimination of one or more full-time change clerks. It was assumed that this equipment would cost approximately $12,000 per year in rental costs and maintenance and result in $26,700 per year savings if one full-time change clerk at $3 per hour could be eliminated.

The total cost of improvements recommended under the Phase IV plan for the redevelopment of the Broad and Columbia station would cost approximately $1.1 to $1.5 million. The return on this investment, largely in terms of increased ridership and fares and decreased manpower required to run the station, was estimated to be on the order of $139,000 per year.

In addition, SEPTA will be able to maintain a considerably higher standard of station cleanliness as a result of the proposed improvements while the annual labor expense will remain the same for the normal maintenance program. There will also be some long-term maintenance economies, because items made of stainless steel require less maintenance than items made of wood or wrought iron; new turnstiles will require fewer service calls; fluorescent lighting less frequent bulb replacement; and so forth.

3. *Community benefits.* In general, improved lighting, appearance, and safety features will attract more people to subway stations, which, in turn, will help to increase adjacent property values, reduce street congestion, and generally uplift the perceived quality of life in the area. Perhaps the most striking impact of subway appearance is a negative one when stations are allowed to become run down. A study was done on the subway partronage at five run-down Philadelphia subway stations on one line, as compared to bus transit following the same basic

route. It was found that subway ridership averaged 13 percent less than that of buses, despite the overcrowded conditions and longer travel time of the latter mode. When all phases of the proposed subway station improvement project are completed, it is anticipated that many of the passengers who have been lost to the bus lines will return to using the stations. A conservative estimate has placed a total number of daily riders using the stations after the improvements are completed at 56,000 a day.[18]

Summary

The Philadelphia Transit Commission's subway station renovation program was intended to improve the subway's ridership appeal. User benefits include greater safety from accidents and crimes because of lighting improvements and platform modifications; greater provision of riding information and aesthetic appeal; reduced congestion in entrances, exits, and platforms, which in turn improves speed of the transit service; and greater safety through pedestrian bridging. Benefits to the PTC will be derived from increased ridership and revenues, and decreased maintenance and operating costs of the station facilities. Community benefits include improved economic activity and increased property values adjacent to subway stations, reduced street congestion, and improved overall street appearance.

Benefits not discussed above with regard to subway station improvements include:

1. Equality of access for the aged, the poor, and the young. Little specific data were available on the impact of improved subway stations on these users; however, the provision of safer, more accessible stations is expected to be of special benefit to the elderly to whom convenience, comfort, and safety are extremely important.
2. Time savings, auto ownership and operating cost savings, benefits to other travelers, airport access, and impact on employment were not covered, because they had only minor bearing on subway improvements. However, subway station design that promotes better traffic flow and less overcrowding is expected to have a definite impact on total perceived time savings by users.

The Cleveland Transit System

General

In 1960, the Cleveland Rapid was the newest and most modern rapid transit system in the country. Opened in 1955, it was 14.9 miles in length and cost $40 million to construct. The "Rapid," with 14 stations, was completely grade separated with all high-level platforms. Each station featured sheltered, off-street feeder bus terminals for convenient connections, as well as convenient parking for "park-n-ride" commuters and "Kiss 'N' Ride" facilities.[19]

The Rapid, in 1960, handled over 60,000 passengers per weekday, with peaks to over 80,000 around the Christmas season. However, it was designed using a new concept to take the bulk of the peak rush-hour pressure off of the highways; and as such, it was arranged to reach out beyond the congested areas of the inner city to intercept commuters as they approached from the outlying suburbs. The Rapid enables them to get to town in 17 minutes instead of 36 minutes which the bus takes. Basic weekday service runs four-car trains at six-minute headways at peak hours, and two-car trains at six-minute headways during the off-peak period. A fixed-fare system is used.

The Need for Improvements

The Cleveland Rapid was built to alleviate peak-hour traffic congestion on approach routes to the urban core. However, it was initially severely handicapped by the lack of adequate and convenient downtown distribution points. It had only one downtown station—Union Terminal on the western edge of the central business district. Because of this, only 21 percent of those working within the business core were within 800 feet of that station, making it necessary for many Rapid commuters to transfer to and from buses within the CBD.

The lack of more convenient distribution points, plus the crowded conditions of the single station that did exist, kept the patronage of the Rapid below its potential. It was estimated that 52,000 people would use the Rapid by 1975, despite the single CBD distribution point. However, consultants also estimated that if a distribution subway loop were constructed, 123,000 passengers per average weekday would use the subway by 1975. It was estimated that 17,000 local passenger trips would be served by the loop, making total weekday usage 140,000 as compared to 76,000 if no changes were made in the system.

Plans for a Euclid Avenue extension and downtown distribution loop were prepared in such a way as to eliminate other weak points in the existing system. For example, the Cleveland system needed to extend more lines to suburban areas in order to better fulfill its primary objective of cutting off traffic on heavily traveled approach routes, especially to the northeast. Another need was for an extension to connect Hopkins Airport directly to the downtown area. Cleveland's problem involving airport access is somewhat unique. Even though the airport is small compared to other major airports (3,100 employees at Hopkins compared with 35,000 at Kennedy Airport in New York) and there is relatively little delay for passengers taking highway vehicles to the airport, a large percentage of air travelers have destinations in Cleveland suburbs served by rapid transit. Since there was no through service connecting the Hopkins Airport, people would drive and not use the CTS at all.

Benefits of the Downtown Loop and Extensions

1. *User benefits*. The principal benefit of the new downtown loop was the increased accessibility of commercial and cultural centers; the secondary benefit was increased patronage. However, it was determined that the downtown distribution would add immeasurably to the usefulness of Cleveland's rapid transit by taking people closer to their points of destination without the necessity of transferring within the CBD. The three proposed subway stations on the Euclid Avenue loop will bring four times as many rapid transit riders within only 800 feet of major commercial facilities as the single station arrangement.

A new rapid transit extension to Shaker Heights, built on the center strip of the northeast freeway, was to be five miles long with five stations and cost a little over $11 million. It was estimated that riders on this line would have an 11-15-minute time savings per trip to the central city area. Table 4-2 summarizes the number of daily riders estimated to benefit from the new line.

Benefits to users of the airport extension would be high frequency, greater dependability, and time savings. The latter benefit would occur largely as a result of the airport extension's connecting directly with lines to other suburbs, so that travelers from those suburbs could make a quick, smooth transition to downtown.

2. *Community benefits*. Fifty percent of airport-bound riders originate in the Cleveland suburbs, 30 percent from the Shaker Heights area and 20 percent

Table 4-2
Summary of Rider Estimates for the Shaker Heights Extension

Source	Daily Riders	
Diverted from Automobiles		
Trips to CBD only*	1,843	
Trips to areas other than CBD	461	
Sub Total		2,304
Diverted from CTS Bus Routes		
Route 55	2,155	
Route 80	471	
Sub Total		2,626
Grand Total of riders diverted		4,930

*Represents a 29 percent diversion factor which Cleveland had experienced previously on other similar extensions.

from Windermere Station in northeastern Cleveland. Without the airport link, these passengers would very likely drive to the airport. Thus, in terms of auto diversion and other passengers, the following projections were made for the airport extension project:

a. 583 daily auto riders from the CBD would be diverted to the new extension.
b. 231 other auto riders would be diverted.
c. 150 passengers from the one bus line would be diverted.
d. 540 airline employees and passengers would use the extension.
e. 799 other daily passengers, including employees of plants along the route, sightseers, and others, would be diverted.

The total estimated number of airport passengers was projected to be 2,294. After the line was opened in 1968, actual riders were over 4,000 per day—indicating overwhelming success of the line.

Aside from this success, an important finding resulting from the project was that the peaking characteristics for airport travelers were different from those of the journey-to-work commuters. As is commonly experienced, 40 to 50 percent of all daily commuters normally crowd the rapid transit system during the two peak periods between 8 and 10 in the morning and 4 and 6 in the evening each work day. In contrast to this, the airport traveler peaks were found to be relatively flat, with slightly higher volumes at midday and again at 10 P.M., and with the volume on weekends similar to that during weekdays, whereas the rest of the system is relatively idle on weekends. The effect of the airport-related ridership patterns is particularly helpful in filling unused system capacity during off-peak hours, creating greater system revenues at no extra cost in terms of increased capacity. To this extent, passengers may benefit in the long run by lower fares, since the greater revenue from off-peak airport service will help defray total operating costs.[20]

Summary

The Cleveland Transit System's downtown loop and suburban extensions benefit users through improved access to commercial and cultural facilities because of better downtown passenger distribution; time savings of 11 to 15 minutes on the northeast extension; and time savings and the convenience of high frequency service for the airport extension. The operator enjoys increased patronage, creating fuller utilization of existing capacity, and because of the airport extension, obtains more off-peak utilization of the whole transit system. Community benefits include reduced auto congestion because of rail access to the airport for a larger number of air travelers and a significant reduction of auto utilization by other riders. Benefits to users not discussed include equality of access, safety, and automobile cost savings for which specific information was lacking. Further, impact on employment, land use, and the environment were treated implicitly in improved downtown access and reduced auto congestion. Other information on these effects was not available, since the extensions were designed primarily to obtain fuller realization of benefits from the existing system.

The Washington Metropolitan Area Transit Authority

General

The WMATA regional system, a new high-speed rapid transit system, is now under construction. The first phase of the system is 25 miles in length and has 31 stations. It consists of two main trunk lines, one connecting Pentagon City in Arlington with Kenilworth in the eastern part of Washington (across the Anacostia River), and the other connecting Van Ness in northwest D.C. with Silver Spring, Maryland, just across the northeast D.C. boundary. The two lines will cross at Metrocenter Station in Central Washington.[21]

The basic 25-mile system—which will eventually grow to a 97-mile and 86-station regional system—is expected to be complete by 1975 and will cost an estimated $425 million. It will be a state-of-the-art system with many technological innovations including fully air-conditioned stations, computer-monitored automatic fare collection systems, a completely automatic train control (ATC) and communications system, a hazard detection system, and the most modern vehicle equipment available.

Need for the WMATA Regional System

The primary need for the adopted regional system is to relieve downtown congestion during rush hours and during the numerous special celebrations and seasonal events occurring each year in the District. Washington is a tourist city, and its growing traffic problem is choking off the District's access arteries, particularly across the Potomac River in the west and the Anacostia River in the east.

Secondly, more efficient planning and utilization of economic resources, including land, is necessary. Washington's industry is becoming increasingly decentralized, with manufacturing and many government institutions moving to the suburbs. At the same time, most of the low-skilled labor pool for these industries is still located in the inner city and is experiencing growing under-employment. Therefore, a way is needed to create a reverse flow of commuters so that industries in the suburbs will have a larger supply of labor, and workers in the city will again have access to job opportunities. Likewise many commercial, retail, governmental, and professional service offices are still located in the core of the District, and more efficient transportation is needed to bring employees into the downtown area.

The people of Washington envision a growing need to create a better, more effective link, not only between complementary industries, services, and institutions, but also between cultural, recreational and educational facilities.[22] Traffic congestion and tourist parking have created a tremendous barrier for the residents of the metropolitan region who wish to take advantage of local cultural, recreational and educational facilities. The new transit could alleviate these barriers and promote greater utilization of the available facilities and activities.

Benefits of the Adopted Regional System to
the Washington, D.C., Metropolitan Area

In their study to determine the economic feasibility of the WMATA system, Development Research Associates calculated that, in terms of 1968 dollars, the cumulative benefits of the new rapid rail transit system to users through the year 2020 would be almost $3 billion.[23] This figure, when compared with the present value of project costs of $.95 billion, results in a benefit-cost ratio of 3.2. A summary of benefits to the year 1990 is found in Table 4-3.

Table 4-3
Summary of Quantifiable Benefits

The annual benefits by 1990, in 1968 constant dollars, are:	
Constant Transit Users	$ 82,920,600
Diverted Auto Drivers and Passengers	
Time savings to peak period commuters	11,130,000
Operating cost savings	11,638,700
Parking cost savings to peak period commuters	15,441,100
Insurance cost savings to commuters	2,177,700
Additional vehicle savings	17,908,400
Non-Diverted Peak Period Motorists	36,750,000
Business Community	
Trucking Industry	4,620,000
Suburban Employers	3,484,000*
Total	$186,070,500

*The value obtained for βi was annualized for the period 1972 to 1990 on the basis of incremental work trips.

Source: Development Research Associates.

1. *User benefits*

Time Savings. Most of the benefits accruing directly to users were calculated in terms of peak period commuters because of the basic assumption that the transit system is principally designed to expedite rush-hour traffic. Theoretically, then, estimates for the dollar value of time saved are conservative and would be higher if savings to all riders had been included. In a report by Alan M. Voorhees & Associates, Inc., the value of time saved per passenger was assumed to be $2.31/hour or $.0385/minute.[24] This figure was derived from studies by the Bureau of Public Roads on the dollar value of time saved for alternative highway systems, based on average hourly rates for the area. The monetary equivalent of the time-saving benefits for constant users was calculated to be approximately $82.9 million.

Benefits to motorists diverted to transit. Development Research Associates has developed projections on the automobile operating, parking, and insurance cost savings which would accrue to automobile owners and passengers who are diverted to the WMATA transit system. Their results were based on the costs presented in Table 4-4. Total monetary savings may be seen by referring back to Table 4-3.

Equality of access. The new rapid rail transit system will greatly improve access to employment opportunities throughout the region. The greatest impact will most probably be in providing "reverse haul" service, which presently is largely nonexistent.[c] Development Research Associates reported that:

The lack of reverse haul service combined with the present trends of employment location and low income residences has created, in part, high "sub-employment" rates in the inner city. A recent United Planning Organization survey, for example, showed that two-thirds of the unemployed in the Cardoza area were unemployed because they could not get to existing job opportunities.

At the same time, however, a survey conducted for the purpose of gathering firm pledges of jobs from employers of retail and industrial centers and suburban government institutions has shown that a significant number of employment opportunities does exist in at least 20 locations outside the city. Table 4-5 shows how the new transit system will directly, or through feeder bus service, serve the major employment centers outside of the CBD.

In addition, the WMATA system will also provide access to educational, cultural, and health facilities. This aspect is particularly important to the young (under 15) and the elderly (over 60) who, in 1970, comprised 39.9 percent of the inner-city population, and were projected to increase to 45.3 by 1990.

2. *Operator benefits.* The new WMATA system will be one of the most

---

[c]Reverse haul service refers to providing transportation for low-income inner-city residents to the semiskilled and unskilled job opportunities which, due to the decentralization of many retail and manufacturing firms, are now located in the suburbs away from the downtown area.

Table 4-4
Costs of Operating an Automobile[a] (Baltimore 1967 Prices)

	Cost per Mile
Variable Costs	
Repairs and Maintenance	$.0176
Accessories	.0008
Replacement Tires and Tubes	.0023
Gasoline	.0150
Oil	.0023
Miscellaneous Taxes	.0095
	$.0475
Fixed Costs	
Depreciation	$.0281
Insurance	.0142
Garage, Parking, Tolls	.0180
Registration and Fixed Costs	.0024
	$.0627

Adjusting to 1968 Washington Variable Costs[b]

1 Baltimore to Washington Adjustment   (To account for difference
   .0475 x 1.0194 = .04842   in cost of living)

2 May 1967 to May 1968 Inflation Adjustment
   .04842 x 1.0213 = .0495 Variable

Sources:

[a]U.S. Department of Transportation.
[b]Development Research Associates.

modern rapid transit systems in the world, designed for failsafe operations. It will be completely automated, which will greatly reduce operating and crew costs. Also, since all scheduling and operating strategies will be determined by computer, there will be a minimum of lost efficiency due to human error.

3. *Community benefits.* Benefits to the general public that were considered quantifiable by Development Research Associates were classified by those accruing to nondiverted auto drivers and the business community. These are:

a. *Nondiverted peak-period motorists.* These drivers include tourists and business commuters who are expected to save time and have a safer, more comfortable trip due to less congestion on access highways. These benefits were calculated to be worth approximately $36,750 million per year by 1990.

b. *Business community.* The benefits due to decreased congestion were calculated as accruing largely to the trucking industry, because their drivers can cover more territory and can operate more efficiently, and to suburban employers, who would have smaller requirements to provide parking facilities for the reverse commuter.

Table 4-5

Level of Service Provided by Adopted Regional System to Existing Potential Employment Areas in the Suburbs

	Directly Served	Served with Feeder Bus	Not Served
Retail Shopping Centers			
Tysons Corner		X	
Seven Corners		X	
Bethesda	X		
Korvettes		X	
Montgomery Mall		X	
Wheaton Plaza	X		
Silver Spring	X		
Prince Georges Plaza	X		
Crystal Plaza	X		
Marlow Hts.		X	
Industrial Areas			
Ardmore Area	X		
Landover Area	X		
Shirley Industrial Park	X		
Federal Agencies			
Goddard Space Flight		X	
Agriculture Research		X	
Atomic Energy			X*
Bureau of Standards			X*
Bureau of Census	X		
Pentagon	X		
NIH	X		

*Will be served with proposed extensions.
Source: Development Research Associates.

The benefits to the trucking industry were based on time savings and on an average hourly wage for truck drivers of $4.53/hour and were computed to total $4.6 million annually. The benefits to suburban employers, based in part on the cost of land acquisition and parking lot resurfacing costs, were computed to be $3.5 million annually by 1990.

Summary

The Washington Metropolitan Area Transit Authority (WMATA) is a regional system now under construction. Its planners envision significant time savings for peak-hour commuters, with an estimated value of $82.9 million. In addition, automobile operation, parking, and insurance cost savings will accrue to passengers switching to rapid transit. Better access to employment will be possible, especially for inner-city residents who travel to the expanded suburban job market, and users will have better access to educational, cultural, and health facilities. WMATA expects to have low operating costs due to automated operations, with a minimum dependence upon human effort. Community benefits will include reduced auto congestion, providing nontransit-using motorists with time savings and greater safety and comfort; reduced costs of surface distribution, especially trucking; and reduced costs to suburban employers in providing parking facilities.

In general, the benefits of WMATA are greater mobility and lowered travel and travel-related costs. Specific treatment of land use and environmental impact was not included for lack of information.

The Chicago Transit Authority Subway Expansion Program

General

In 1968, the Chicago Transit Authority began planning for a major expansion program. The program consisted of two principal components: (i) an east-west high-level shuttle or "distributor" subway, extending from the University of Illinois circle campus to two CTA branches along the lake front; and (ii) a conventional loop subway to replace an older elevated structure that followed four major downtown arteries. The cost of the proposed project, as estimated in 1968 was $278 million.[25] Engineering plans call for completion of the construction by 1978.

In 1965, as initial planning for the new subway neared completion, it was determined that simply replacing the old elevated line and extending the system to the north and south would not produce the maximum number of benefits. Although it was hoped that removing the ugly elevated structure would make blighted commercial areas more attractive for redevelopment, the distribution of riders within certain growing commercial areas became a problem. Therefore, it was then decided to include plans for a high-level distributor subway, in addition to the conventional loop, in order to give riders from those key areas of growth more convenient access to the main system.

Need for the Central Area Subway

It is estimated that by 1975, 332,000 persons will travel to the central city area daily. Of these, 270,000 will use the transit system. By 1990, these numbers are expected to increase to 394,000 and 316,000 respectively. These estimates only include travel to the CBD, however; so total travel, including outbound passengers, should be approximately twice the above. During the peak hours, more than 60 percent of these people will use public transit. (The maximum historical accumulation figure for Chicago is 85 percent of all daily passengers arriving by subway during the same peak period.)

Chicago's planning policies also stress the commercial use of land. It is hoped that the new subway plan will not only alleviate the need for new downtown highways and parking lots in order to stimulate new commercial development, but will also free up existing downtown areas for such development. Over one billion dollars of new development has been added to the Chicago center business district since 1968, and land is becoming an ever scarcer commodity.

In addition, Chicago has had a growing need to find employment opportunities for underprivileged people, accompanied by the need to give people in depressed areas more mobility to take advantage of Chicago's social, cultural, and educational facilities.

Benefits of the Proposed Central Area
Subway System

1. *User benefits.* As mentioned earlier, the improved rapid transit system will carry 270,000 persons daily to the central business district in 1975 and 315,000 in 1990. It has been estimated, too, that the improved system will save commuters 15,000 man-hours daily in 1975 and 25,000 in 1990. Using a value of 1.5 cents per passenger minute saved or 90 cents per hour saved, and 250 working days per year (similar to the estimates for the value of time savings for the new San Francisco Bay Area Rapid Transit), Chicago commuters will save $337.5 million a year in travel time in 1975 and $562.5 million in 1990.

In 1975 the distributor system alone is expected to serve the 115,000 persons who enter the central area each day during peak hour via rapid transit and commuter trains. In 1990 this total is expected to increase to 152,000 and total daily distributor passengers entering and leaving the area will be twice these volumes. Estimates for time savings from the distributor system are 10 minutes for passengers transferring from commuter rail service and two minutes for those transferring from rapid transit. The passengers entering the central area via transit represent 83 percent of all commuters entering during peak hours, the remainder entering by auto. Estimated passenger volumes on the distributor will be considerably increased by local ridership, those making secondary intra-central area trips, and those who make the main trip into the central area by modes other than commuter trains or rapid transit. Estimates for the volume of these passengers have not been made.

2. *Community benefits.* In terms of capital investment cost and land utilization, the following summary of the system's benefits was made during a 1970 congressional hearing:

There are some traffic engineers who already have recommended the banning of automobiles completely from the central area. More than 20 years ago Chicago had the foresight to build an expressway while reserving the median strip of its right-of-way for rapid transit. I wish that members of this committee could come to Chicago and observe—especially during the rush hours—the speed of the rapid transit lines while automobiles are practically at a standstill.

Just to accommodate the automobiles of those now using the rapid transit in one expressway median strip during peak hours would call for construction of a 12-lane expressway—six lanes in each direction—in addition to the present eight lanes. Not only is this system providing a great service to the passengers and motorists of the city and suburbs on the West Side, but there is a tremendous saving in costs. Conservatively speaking, the cost of constructing 12 new expressway lanes would be more than $200 million. The cost of installing the rapid transit system in the right-of-way when built was approximately $20 million, borne by a city of Chicago bond issue.[26]

In addition, evaluations of the potential economic impact of the subway improvement program on real estate values and employment resulted in the following projections:

a. It was estimated that the value of real property in the primary impact area could increase by more than $1.8 million by 1990, assuming the new system is in operation by 1975. The estimated immediate increase in property values when the new loop was constructed was $217 million.[d] In order to arrive at these figures, estimates were made of the increased value of land in which new construction has taken place, and the value of new improvements and innovations that would not have taken place without the transit improvements—including the value of new residential construction and the increased value of land adjacent to the new construction.

b. The gross tax revenues from this increase in property values will be an amount equivalent to the total cost of the proposed improvement over a period of 10 years. Furthermore, if no improvement were made, there would be very little property value increase but a substantial cost to maintain the old elevated structure.

c. The new system will take advantage of and stimulate prime development areas. In particular, the razing of the old elevated structure is expected to significantly alter patterns of commercial development. In total, commercial space within the central area is expected to increase 17 percent between 1966 and 1975, and another 12 percent by 1985 to 161.6 million square feet. Of this, 62 million square feet—an increase of 19 million over 1966—will be for office space, representing a new demand of about one million square feet per year, 30 percent of which is attributable to additional employment, 48 percent to the increase in space per employee, and 22 percent to the replacement of space.

d. Projections of employment, assuming the implementation of the new system, show an increase of employment of 97,400, while, without the system, employment is expected to increase by only 75,000—a difference of 22,300

[d]Based on projections made by the Chicago Transit Authority.

jobs. This amounts to an increase in the growth rate of employment of roughly 29 percent. Certain assumptions were applied by the Chicago Transit Authority to arrive at these figures:

1. Employment in the Chicago Standard Metropolitan Statistical Area (SMSA) will continue to grow at a rate similar to that of previous CTA projections.
2. Developers of new office structures in the Central Area will be able to market new office space, under construction or planned, within a reasonable time period following the completion of each development.
3. The addition of new office space in the Central Area will cause a reduction in employment density. That is, as new office space comes on the market, some firms will shift from the old space to the new and some remaining firms will expand their space.
4. Buildings in fair or poor condition will tend to lose employment at a higher rate than those which are in good or excellent condition.
5. Buildings in poor or fair condition which have prime locations are more apt to maintain higher occupancy rates, but on the other hand are more likely to be demolished at a faster rate than comparable buildings in less desirable locations. Employment will, therefore, remain relatively stable or increase significantly over time in the established prime locations in the Central Area.

   e. Perhaps the biggest benefit of improved transit facilities is to reduce downtown congestion, and to increase the mobility of underprivileged persons. These benefits are summarized in a speech delivered by Chicago resident, Ralph Petratos:

... Congestion on our city streets and expressways, and the resulting air pollution caused by the stop-and-go driving of thousands of cars and trucks is slowly strangling the life-line of our urban centers. As a former employee of the State of Illinois Emergency Traffic patrol, I have first hand knowledge of the following facts:

- A hardship is imposed on the breadwinner in a family who has to spend a considerable length of time travelling to and from work and in travelling for shopping. An inadequate public mass transportation system means that often people in low income brackets, because they cannot afford new cars have two inadequate vehicles in various stages of disrepair—one for transportation of the breadwinner—primary source of income in a family and the other for the use of the family. When one or both finally give out, they are abandoned on the streets to be replaced by other cars of similar vintage.
- In the Lawndale area alone, where I reside, there is an average of three or four abandoned cars per city block per month. This condition hinders street cleaning and a healthy environment.
- The Dan Ryan Expressway which extends from 95th Street on the South side to the Loop, services an area where 750,000 persons reside. Included in this group is about 100,000 residents who fall in the low income bracket and reside in high-rise apartments built and managed by the Chicago Housing Authority. Many of these people are totally dependent on the Chicago

Transit Authority for transportation as they go about their lawful occupations. Imagine, if you can, the utter chaos on our city expressways and streets if the riders who now use the Chicago Transit Authority were transported by automobile. There are not enough lanes on our expressways to accommodate this volume of traffic, and there would not be enough parking facilities to handle them. To many inner city residents, because of the lack of adequate public transportation, an automobile is a necessary evil. The average low income family is often pushed to the brink of bankruptcy by automobile ownership because of the high cost of upkeep. In most cases, they are forced to purchase second-rate, second-hand vehicles, from shady dealers who deal with shyster finance companies. The cost of repairs and the insurance rates are sky-rocketing and often the purchases of license plates and vehicle stickers put a severe strain on the family budget. Improved and extended mass transportation services could eliminate the need for a substantial portion of automobile ownership for poor families who can ill afford such vehicles.[27]

Summary

The Chicago Transit Authority's proposed subway expansion program is not yet completed, but its principal user benefit will be time savings over the existing system. The CTA also expects to obtain the advantage of an increased passenger volume for the whole system. Community benefits include expected real property value increases totaling $1.8 billion in 15 years; gross tax revenues generated from the increased values equal in 10 years to the improvement costs (without reflecting savings in maintenance costs); creation of substantial amounts of new office space available to increase employment potential as well as replace less desirable space and permit allocation of more space per employee; addition of 22,000 jobs, or a 29 percent increase in the employment growth rate; and major improvements in the access of disadvantaged downtown residents to employment and to commercial and civic facilities.

Benefits not discussed above are vehicle operating costs and operator benefits in maintenance costs and crime prevention for which information was lacking; and benefits to other travelers and the environment which were not specifically relevant.

The Massachusetts Bay Transportation Authority

General

The Massachusetts Bay Transportation Authority (MBTA) was organized out of the old Massachusetts Transit Authority (MTA) in 1966 in order to incorporate the 77 surrounding towns and communities into a comprehensive planning framework to be financed by public and federal funds. The MTA's jurisdiction at the time of transition consisted of only 14 cities and towns and had four major subway routes with 23 miles of track. At that time, it also operated six streetcar routes with 35 miles of double track, only eight of which ran over city streets.

When the MBTA was formed, it began work on a master plan to include bus and commuter train service for the entire metropolitan region. Under the policy of providing a balanced transportation system, the first stage of the master plan was to develop a list of high priority projects designated as the Immediate Action Program. Under the assumption that most people would rather park than drive, the objective of the MBTA was to work with highway planners to develop a dual-mode scheme whereby most commuters would drive part of the way, park, and then take the rapid transit or one of the three MBTA-supported commuter lines which made up almost 200 miles of regional commuter service. In this way, the MBTA planned to augment rather than replace private car travel. One of these lines—the Old Colony line, which extended to 15 cities on the South Shore of the Massachusetts Bay—was to be converted to the South Shore Rapid Transit Extension which is now in operation.

The $340 million Immediate Action Program basically included the following concepts:

1. A 2.5 mile, $59.8 million extension of the Dorchester-Cambridge rail line to the northwest toward Arlington to meet Route 2, a major commuter highway.
2. A new 15 mile South Shore extension of the Cambridge-Dorchester line to South Weymouth along the road bed of the Old Colony line at a cost of $66.8 million (including $2.5 million for right of way). This would serve as an alternative to the heavily traveled Route 3 for South Shore commuters.
3. The relocation and extension of the Everett line to another existing rail route to northeast Boston, a distance of 6.6 miles at a cost of $75 million.
4. A 1.1 mile extension of a trolley line to Somerville in the north.
5. A southerly extension of the Everett-Malden (North-South) line of 2.5 miles through Roxbury to a major parkway.
6. $39 million for new streetcars to service the westbound line, and $20 million for new rapid transit cars for the eastbound line.

At the same time and in the spirit of marketing rapid transit, the MBTA planned a $15.1 million station renovation program and also planned for ample parking space at terminal stations in hopes of luring commuters out of their cars.[28] Although transit facilities already existed, the MBTA considered building a new system to extend service; however, this idea proved to be infeasible. Boston, the American pioneer in rapid transit, developed its first line in 1897, which until 1960 was totally controlled by private, profit-oriented interests. As such, the system became a hodgepodge of dissimilar and noninterchangeable equipment containing every type of conveyance available except a cable car—buses, rail diesel cars, diesel locomotives, motor buses, trackless trolleys, two types of street cars, and four different types of subway cars ranging from 48 footers for 44 passengers to 70 footers for 200 passengers.

The Need for Transit Improvement and Expansion in Boston

Upgrading service, therefore, is a problem because existing track, tunnel, and station design are not compatible with the newer, longer, and faster transit equipment now available. In order to eventually overcome this problem, the MBTA is now attempting to replace existing antiquated systems wherever possible, so as to make the entire system more convenient for passengers by reducing transfer requirements and to facilitate future expansion.[29] Modernization toward the suburbs is considered a high priority for two reasons:

a. Initial efforts were to reduce the traffic burden on the downtown area by diverting auto commuters to transit before they reached the central business district (CBD).
b. Despite its antiquated system, the MBTA has one of the best downtown distributor services in the nation. Therefore, a logical position was to enhance the use of this distributor subway network with greater feeder capacities.

The MBTA learned a tough lesson three years earlier about the value of marketing public transit. At that time it had bought from the New Haven Railroad some existing right of way to the west of Boston through Newton Falls, and put into service old but fast subway/surface trolley cars (Presidential Conference or PCC cars) in hopes of luring large numbers of middle-class commuters onto the system from the bedroom communities of Wellesley, Newton, and Chestnut Hill. In so doing, the MBTA hoped to attain 35,000 commuters a day (30,000 a day was the breakeven point). The line, however, has been a failure and at most has achieved only 26,000 passengers per day. It is operating at a $600,000 a year deficit. The reason for this failure has not been the lack of market demand, but simply that the PCC cars are incapable of luring motorists out of their cars. The cars are old and cramped, have poor access and seating, are mechanically unreliable, and require a motorman for each car. This, it was concluded, is not the way to appeal to the vast majority of suburban commuters.

Another indictment of Boston's antiquated rapid transit system was the fact that between 1954 and 1964 ridership dropped by almost 21 percent from 397,714 per day to 314,308 per day.[30] At the same time auto commuter travel rose by 35 percent from 714,398 per day to 965,944 per day, resulting in a traffic catastrophe in Boston in which the slightest disturbance in one part of the city's street system (which is characterized by narrow, aimlessly laid out streets for the most part) may cause traffic snarls all over the city. For example, in 1967 during an unexpected three-inch snowfall in November, there was such a traffic jam in the Hub area that it took a driver four hours to go from Logan Airport to Cambridge, a distance of six miles, and three hours to go from the airport into Boston, a distance of two miles. This is due in part to the rapid commercial development of downtown Boston and in part to the construction of two major new expressways directly into the downtown area. However, it is also caused by the dilapidated and inaccessible state of the rapid transit system that never reached far enough into the growing suburban areas to provide commuters with an easy transfer. This condition has resulted directly from the lack of regional orientation to transportation planning for the Boston area, which is rapidly changing from an industrial to a commercial center; the lack of a viable marketing concept; the lack of a system capable of expanding to meet growing needs;[31] and, mostly, the lack of balanced perspective toward the role of rapid transit as an integral part of Boston's overall transportation fabric.

Another important need for the MBTA's masterplan was to reduce maintenance and operating costs per vehicle mile traveled, which, in 1966, were the highest in the country and almost double those of the nearest competitor, New York City. The antiquated and archaic equipment the MBTA was operating required constant maintenance and excessive operating crews, as compared to that required by newer equipment. In fact, in 1967 when the MBTA bought a fleet of new cars for the Cambridge-Ashmont line, it only required 92 new cars to do the job of 135 old ones.[32]

The operating deficit, however, was not unique to the MBTA in serving the transit needs of the metropolitan region. Several of the railroads operating commuter services, notably the Boston and Maine to the North Shore and the northwest and the New Haven to the South Shore (Old Colony line) were losing money rapidly and threatening to shut down service despite heavy subsidies by the MBTA and the communities which they served. In 1960, when plans for the new South Shore line were begun, the Old Colony line alone was getting almost $1 million per year in subsidies, and the New Haven claimed they actually were losing much more than that.

Benefits of the MBTA Expansion Program

Benefits of the Immediate Action Program are presently starting to be realized, largely due to the nearly completed South Shore extension, one of the first projects undertaken.

1. *User benefits.* The main benefit of the new South Shore extension to users of the service is a faster ride to South Station (where the Old Colony line also terminates) and better distribution to downtown Boston (it connects directly

with the downtown distributor service). The new transit will cost about the same (approximately 50 cents between Quincy and Boston); but it will have more frequent service than the commuter train (three-minute headways at Quincy Station at peak hours versus a minimum of 18-minute headways for the Old Colony), faster running times (7 minutes faster than between Quincy and Boston), and better access with well-planned bus connections and ample parking lots at the suburban end. Initially it was projected that the South Shore extension would attract 25,300 daily riders, 60 percent of whom would be Old Colony commuters. The remaining 40 percent—about 10,000 passengers—were expected to be diverted from the 60,000 people that commute on two major highways to Boston daily.[33]

2. *Operator benefits.* Benefits to the MBTA include the following:

a. Low operating costs for the new system which will have cab signalling and be centrally controlled, thus requiring fewer dispatchers than other lines. The new cars and signalling systems also will result in lower maintenance costs.

b. The new system, with faster and more powerful and reliable cars, will be easier to expand by simply adding extensions and new rolling stock, than older lines with slower, less predictable equipment. This is important since it is projected that the population of the area served by the system will increase 40 percent by 1980.

c. With the broader attractableness of the improved service, if a graduated fare structure is used, the new service may actually pay for itself. Projections show that if patronage targets are surpassed, revenues will completely cover operating costs, including the financing issue.

3. *Community benefits.* Benefits to the general community of the MBTA expansion program are striking indeed. As demonstrated by the South Shore extension project, they include the following:

a. The elimination of a $1 million a year subsidy to the New Haven Railroad to keep the Old Colony commuter service running. (Railroads are paid over $30 million annually for commuter train operating subsidies by the people of Massachusetts—largely to service the greater Boston metropolitan region).

b. New real estate development has taken place in Quincy Center, such as the $100 million State Street Bank complex. It will cover 80 acres, house the bank's computer center, and offer retail shops, a department store, office space and apartment buildings.[34]

c. Commuter traffic on major southeast arteries into Boston will be reduced by 15 percent or more, resulting in less congestion and need for parking in the heart of Boston.

d. More commercial employment opportunities and access to social, cultural, and educational activities in Boston will be available to those living on the South Shore. This is especially important to college-age students (there are more than a quarter of a million in the greater Boston area). Likewise, new housing opportunities south of the city will open up to Boston workers at a time when the housing market in Boston is very tight.

Summary

The Massachusetts Bay Transportation Authority's expansion program has already generated benefits from the South Shore extension. Users are experiencing time savings with rapid transit compared to the former commuter railroad line. Access to the downtown has improved because of the extension's integration with downtown distributor service. Time savings also accrue from better connections at the suburban end. As operator, the MBTA has obtained lower operating costs because of its cab signalling and centrally controlled dispatching systems and lower maintenance costs on the new cars and signalling system. The extension has a simple, low-cost expansion potential, as well as the potential to recover all its operating and financing costs through attraction of sufficient volume and use of a graduated fare structure. This is possible because the right of way was able to be purchased from an existing railroad at nominal cost.

Community benefits include the elimination of a $1 million per year subsidy to the predecessor line; significant new commercial and residential development in South Shore towns, notably Quincy; reduced auto congestion along southeast arteries and in downtown Boston, as well as less need for downtown parking space; greater access to employment opportunities in downtown Boston for South Shore residents; and better access to cultural and educational resources of the center city.

Benefits not discussed above for lack of information were cost savings of automobile operation, increased safety, and environmental impact. Crime prevention was not applicable. Equality of access was not especially relevant for the South Shore line, since major new employment opportunities here had not yet developed before its construction.

5 Bus Transit

Exclusive Bus Lanes

General

An exclusive bus lane is a lane of an existing highway that has been physically separated from the regular flow of traffic and is limited in its use to buses and perhaps automobiles serving organized carpools. The purpose of the lanes is to maximize the movement of multiple-rider vehicles during periods of rush-hour congestion, without making large capital investments for new rights-of-way. Although the concept is not new, the designation of lanes and their subsequent use is a relatively recent innovation in the field of public transit. In the paragraphs that follow, the experiences of two exclusive bus lanes set up under the auspices of the UMTA Demonstration Grant Program are presented.

Shirley Highway

The high-speed exclusive bus lanes on the Shirley Highway, a federal demonstration grant project, were established as the nation's first such lanes. A test of reserved bus lanes on a five-mile section of the Interstate 95 Freeway highway leading into Washington, D.C., from Virginia began in September 1969. Two center lanes, separated from car traffic by physical barriers, are reserved for inbound buses during the morning rush hours.

Passenger Transport reports that during the first four months of the demonstration project, ridership increased from zero to 5,000.[1] In the subsequent four months the service attracted over 2,200 new customers; and in the same period of time, a reduction of 33 percent of car commuter traffic (from 8,405 to 5,566 cars) was noted along the highway during the early morning rush hours.

In addition to the objective of diverting commuters to bus transit during the peak hour period, the project also is focusing on improving mobility for captive riders. A campaign is being planned to disseminate information among the young, elderly, poor, and handicapped on the availability of the service, especially during off-peak hours.[2] Efforts will include the publication of easily understood special maps and schedules. Cooperation of merchants along bus routes will be solicited for refunding part of the bus fare to shoppers. The idea of mailing transit information with monthly welfare checks also is being considered.

Another proposal under review is the possibility of allowing the federally subsidized exclusive bus lanes to be shared by automobiles carrying full carloads as an incentive for people to travel in carpools.[3] Since the express buses use only a portion of the capacity of the two reserved lanes, only minor design changes would be required to permit metering of other traffic into these lanes.

The successful Shirley Highway bus service will encounter a real test when the demonstration grant is expended late in 1974. At that time, the remaining members of the partnership (the local and state governments) will have to carry the financial obligations amounting to at least $1.2 million of the annual cost of operation.[4]

1. *User benefits.* Since the initiation of the Shirley Highway bus service, almost two out of three express bus riders have been "choice" riders (that is, they have access to a car, but take a bus), as compared to a 44 percent average among other bus riders in the metropolitan area.[5] The primary reason for the increased ratio of choice riders was the desire to avoid driving through the traffic-clogged highway—it is acknowledged to be one of the most congested in the country—and to avoid the inconveniences and high costs of parking.

Time savings. While the new colorful, air-conditioned buses play a significant role in stimulating the commuters' interest in the Shirley Highway bus service, the major appeal derives from the large-scale time savings afforded by the service. Almost 30 minute savings in journey-to-work time from Virginia to Washington work locations have been reported.[6] An auto-commuter attitude survey, conducted by *Fortune Magazine* in the Washington, D.C., area, demonstrated the importance which commuters attach to transit time in deciding which transit method to use on their work trip.[7] Sixty percent of the respondents indicated that they would switch to transit if their current round-trip travel time were matched, and an additional 22 percent would switch if there were round-trip time savings ranging from 10 to 60 minutes. The same study also showed that 85 percent of those surveyed had access to public transport for commuting but did not use it.

Reliability. While the time savings made possible by commuting on the Shirley bus system are a decisive factor in its popular acceptance by the patrons, equally significant is the fact that these bus riders have discovered that the buses run on schedule.

2. *Community benefits*

Environmental impact. Starting April 1971, the project was scheduled to receive deliveries every week of about 10 buses equipped with antipollution devices. Thus, these buses emit practically no polluting fumes and are far less noisy than the conventional models.

Less congestion. The diversion of riders from automobiles to the commuting buses has reduced the number of cars on the streets of Washington.

Secretary Volpe estimated that the expressway buses, patronized by 4,000 commuters daily, represented about 2,800 private vehicles that would otherwise have come into the core city.[8]

Lincoln Tunnel Approach to New York

Since its establishment in December 1970, the exclusive bus lane for the Lincoln Tunnel approach has experienced a six percent increase in ridership, representing an additional 2,300 peak morning riders.[9] The bus lane is one of a series of projects being conducted under the federally sponsored North Jersey to mid-Manhattan Urban Corridor Demonstration program. The exclusive east-bound bus lane was created along a two and one half mile stretch of Interstate 495 that ordinarily carries westbound traffic.

The success of the project has resulted in a study currently underway by the New Jersey Department of Transportation on the feasibility of utilizing 9.5 miles of an unused portion of the West Shore railroad right of way exclusively for express buses.[10] This proposed operation, combined with the exclusive bus lane on the Lincoln Tunnel approach, would provide express bus service along a densely populated and congested corridor extending from Bergen County, New Jersey, to mid-Manhattan.

1. *User benefits*

Time savings. It was estimated that during the first year of operations, over 8.5 million persons (in more than 200,000 buses) saved up to 25 minutes each morning by traveling the I-495 exclusive bus lane. A "before and after" survey indicated that average one-way time savings were between 10 and 19 minutes.[11] During the pre-experiment study, the Port of New York Authority forecasted that peak-hour buses would save about six minutes each way, an estimate which experience has proven to be extremely conservative. Nevertheless, based on their projection and given their assumptions, they estimated the monetary equivalents of time savings shown in Table 5-1. The assumptions were:

1. Each bus on the exclusive lane would carry 45 people.
2. The value of commuting time would range between $1.50 and $2.00 per person per hour.
3. Average bus speeds on the exclusive bus lane would vary between 30 and 40 mph.
4. Two-hour weekday morning peak period bus volume on the exclusive lane would reach 880 by 1970.

Quality of service. To some 95 percent of the patrons, bus service on the exclusive lane also resulted in more reliable travel, and 86 percent considered their daily trip as more enjoyable.[12]

Table 5-1
Range of Annual Road User Benefits

			Annual Benefits		
	% of Eastbound Underpass Buses Using Exclusive Bus Lane		Current Volume 30 m.p.h., $1.50/ hr. (lowest end of benefit range)	Future Volume 40 m.p.h., $2.00/ hr. (highest end of benefit range)	Average
Scheme	Fully	Partially			
1	60%		$390,000	$ 860,000	$625,000
2	60%	25%	430,000	1,010,000	720,000
3	60%	40%	470,000	1,120,000	795,000
4	75%	25%	480,000	1,140,000	810,000
5	100%		510,000	1,210,000	860,000

Source: The Port of New York Authority, *A Plan for an Exclusive Bus Lane on Interstate Route 495 from the New Jersey Turnpike to the Lincoln Tunnel*, January 1967, pp. 11-12.

2. *Operator benefits*

Increased safety. Survey results indicate that since the start-up of the exclusive bus lane, 85 percent of the bus drivers feel more relaxed and 75 percent feel safer while driving to Manhattan.

Improved traffic flow. It was found that substantial improvements were attained in terms of bus movement as well as flow of other eastbound traffic in the morning peak period. Traveling on the exclusive bus lane saved each bus an average of over 10 minutes of travel time one way. In addition, the vehicular capacity of the normal eastbound traffic lanes was increased; the bus lane carried over 10 times the number of people transported in any of the other three eastbound lanes and at a faster speed.

The average flow during the morning peak period (between 7:30 and 9:30 A.M.) was 809 buses carrying about 34,000 people. The averages for the 8:00 to 9:00 A.M. period were 480 buses and 21,100 passengers. Further, in May 1971, during the transportation emergency created by the nationwide railroad strike, a record flow of 597 buses with 25,800 passengers in the 8:00 to 9:00 A.M. period and 1,096 buses with 47,800 passengers in the peak period was achieved.[13] Of added significance, the exclusive bus lane was able to handle the increased loads without stoppages or delays.

3. *Benefits to other travelers.* A majority of the New York-bound motorists felt that their driving conditions also were improved. The same observation was voiced even by many of the westbound motorists, despite the fact that one of their lanes was converted to the bus lane running in the opposite direction.

Summary

Freeway lanes reserved exclusively for express buses bound for the CBD during peak hours can mean significant time savings for commuters, as has been demonstrated by the experiments on Shirley Highway (Northern Virginia) and the Lincoln Tunnel approach (New York).

For the riders who have switched from commuting by car, the savings on parking and operating costs can be substantial. Moreover, it may no longer be necessary for their families to own a second car. The disappearance from the rush-hour highway traffic of the cars previously driven by the new bus passengers can be sizable enough so that the traffic flow on the rest of the lanes also is increased.

Further, the time savings achieved allow increased recirculation of the bus fleet for the operator. Because new, attractive buses are normally employed in these programs in order to appeal to choice riders (that is, those who have automobiles available for commutation), and these buses as well as other traffic move faster, the amount of fumes and pollutants emitted is reduced. The reduction in the number of automobiles brought onto the city streets similarly contributes to less air and noise pollution.

During off-peak hours these exclusive lane commuter buses may be applied to transporting the riders who lack mobility, such as the elderly, persons without any automobile, the young, and the handicapped. Such a program has been proposed by the operator of the Shirley Highway express buses.

Although the carrying capacity of the highway is substantially increased through reserved lanes for buses, it is possible to achieve an even further increase by admitting car pools—private automobiles carrying a full load—to the exclusive lane. The maximum advantages of exclusive bus lanes, however, may be realized when combined with express bus service. This latter topic is discussed under the section "Express Buses" in this chapter.

Dial-A-Ride

General

The Dial-A-Ride concept is based on a demand-responsive system of public transportation. It differs from traditional taxi service in that several riders with different origins and destinations can be carried at any one time. One of the most difficult problems in implementing the concept is that of maximizing the routing efficiency of the vehicles (generally a form of minibus). Although there are some ongoing efforts to improve the state of the art in routing through the use of computer programs, the potential inherent in the Dial-A-Ride concept has not yet been fully demonstrated. Thus far, however, a few modifications of the concept have been put into service, and these have called for extremely careful planning and progressive management in order to be successful.

Modified Dial-A-Ride Experiment in
Mansfield, Ohio

The Ford Motor Company and a Mansfield Transit operator initiated a modified Dial-A-Ride experimental operation in Mansfield, Ohio. On a single route, served by one bus, a potential rider contacts the driver by radio telephone. If his (the driver's) schedule permits, he will deviate from his fixed route as much as four blocks in order to pick up the caller. Also patrons on the bus can request doorstep discharge. The doorstep service, however, is offered only within several blocks of a fixed, radial, downtown-oriented route.

During the first two months of operation, a 15 percent increase in patronage and a 30 percent increase in revenue was observed.[14] Patrons who request doorstep service pay an additional 50 cents per trip.

Experiments in Peoria, Illinois, and Flint, Michigan

Two federally financed experiments have been initiated in Peoria, Illinois, and Flint, Michigan. In Peoria a door-to-door bus service, linking residences with the large Caterpillar Tractor plant, has been highly successful; after a year of operation, revenues covered the total cost of operation. Each bus made two round trips a day, serving work shifts that began and ended 45 minutes apart. The success of the service is partly attributed to careful market research, route planning, and attention to customer service. Despite the availability of free parking at the plant, 72 percent of the bus riders are those who switched from driving their own cars.

The Merrick Minibus Program

A two-year demonstration project (October 1967 to October 1969) tested the economic viability of an attractive, inexpensive small-bus feeder commuter service in an area of low population density. The demonstration was sponsored by the town of Hempstead in Long Island and financed partly by a grant from UMTA and partly by a local bus line. It serviced 52 percent of the work force living within the project area who commuted to New York City via the Long Island Railroad. The minibus met each outgoing morning and incoming evening commuter train at the Merrick Long Island Railroad Station. During noncommuter hours the buses served the Merrick (an unincorporated community within the Town of Hempstead) business district and a regional shopping center.

Before the start of the service, 41.9 percent of the respondents in a survey had driven to the station and parked their cars; 27.4 percent had been driven to and from the station; 4.8 percent had used carpools; and the remaining 25.9 percent had walked or taken taxis.[15]

During the two years of the project 313,477 persons patronized the minibus system. However, this level of patronage was not high enough to make the service profitable for a private transit operator. The difficulty in bringing patronage up to the breakeven point was attributed to the low-density development pattern of the project area, which is a medium- to high-income residential community. The cost differential between owning a second car and patronizing public transit was not sufficient to attract a significant number of residents to the system.

1. *User benefits.* In the case of the Merrick minibus demonstration project, the service was designed to eliminate the need for a second car, by providing an inexpensive and relatively frequent feeder service. The fare to the railroad station was 25 cents, as compared to taxi fares ranging from 50 cents to $1. Although the commuter service program was unable to generate sufficient patronage to justify a continued operation by the private mass transit company, the experiment has shown a consistently high patronage by teenagers during nonschool periods, particularly Saturday. This finding highlights the need of young people for a reliable, inexpensive means of transit. Saturday seat utilization for the two-year demonstration period averaged 137.4 percent with a peak of 220.5 percent recorded in September, 1968.[16] The minibus program operator has consequently continued this portion of the service.

2. *Community benefits.* In addition to meeting the transportation needs of the poor, this mode of public transit also may serve as a significant source of employment for the poor. Dial-A-Ride operations would require drivers, mechanics, and other types of maintenance personnel, telephone operators, computer technicians and programmers, budgeting and accounting staff, clerical staff, supervisors, and so forth.

A nationwide shortage of both taxi drivers and bus drivers currently exists, with high turnover rates characterizing both occupations. In some communities Dial-A-Ride service may be provided by an existing unionized transit company which recruits and trains the Dial-A-Ride drivers from among the existing employees. However, in other instances, there may not be an established operator or an established union, so that an alternative manpower training program is required.

Transportation-Employment Project: South
Central and East Los Angeles

Transportation deficiencies have been recognized as a significant component of the general inability for low-income persons to fully participate in job and other opportunities. The research and demonstration project in South Central and East Los Angeles addressed itself to the following three of the pertinent problem areas related to that deficiency:

a. Nonavailability of a transportation system.
b. Limited efficiency and dependability of means.
c. Lack of awareness of means for reaching destination.

Improvements in the conventional transportation system included the establishment of three regularly scheduled bus routes. The Century Boulevard between Lynwood-South Gate and Los Angeles Airport, via Watts, was established in July 1966. This line is now operated as part of the Southern California Rapid Transit System without project funds. A line between East Los Angeles and the industrial concentration in the City of Commerce was operated between 1967 and 1969, but was subsequently discontinued. Thirdly, a bus line was established to serve the newly relocated East Los Angeles State Service Center complex. Full responsibility for running this route was assumed by Eastern Cities Transit, Inc. in March 1970, and the line is in full operation without subsidy.

In addition, the extension and development of flexible-route, small-scale, community-based transportation systems were tested. The objectives were to provide new services which would make accessible to nondriving residents some of the destinations previously reached only by automobile and to supplement existing conventional public transportation service.

The services offered by the project consisted of home-to-work transportation; scheduled service between housing projects in South Los Angeles and East Los Angeles and shopping centers, connecting points not previously linked by public transportation; and transportation services for senior citizens to recreational facilities.

Summary

The Dial-A-Ride concept and its less strict applications, such as the feeder-distribution bus service and publicly organized large-scale car-pooling arrangements, encompass a wide range of benefits in terms of improved transportation availability. The specific cases cited in this section noted several types of accruing benefits.

Since the basic idea underlying this concept is to provide direct links between origin and destination as dictated by demand, one of the foremost benefits from its application involves achieving equality of access for those areas and persons who would otherwise remain deprived of mobility. The Merrick minibus project furnished this type of service, providing ready transit to youths in an area principally fashioned for car owners. Improved equality of access would avail the users with a wider choice of job locations, and educational, health, shopping, and recreational facilities. In connection with serving the disadvantaged residents with feeder service, possibilities may be considered for organizing a nonprofit group to run the service in the area.

Direct links mean shorter travel time and greater convenience for those patrons who previously had to combine more than one line or mode of transportation. Riders who were former automobile travelers could realize savings on operating and parking costs as well as car ownership expenditures. Services linking residences and jobs are further exemplified by the Mansfield (Ohio), Peoria (Illinois), and Flint (Michigan) projects.

Availability of ready public transportation supplied by small-bus feeder services not only provides improved transport accessibility to riders but also benefits the operators. The proposed feeder service in the central employment area of Washington, D.C., was designed to eliminate the operator's need to maintain an unnecessarily large fleet of line-haul buses through the adoption of smaller buses to be used in the CBD. The slow congested traffic in this area has reduced the rate of recirculation of the line-haul buses and resulted in a more efficient operation.

Travelers who do not utilize this type of service directly, however, also benefit through improved flow on highways and arterial and local streets. Further, the concept may be suitably applied to airport ground transportation by making access to the airport less cumbersome and costly.

Express Buses

General

Express busing is simply the establishment of through-service along highways, as opposed to local streets and road arteries. Generally, the service runs between a limited number of points or origin and destination, and its routings are designed to serve a particular ridership group such as commuters or shoppers. Three demonstration programs for express busing are described below.

Milwaukee "Freeway Flyer" Express Buses

In April 1964, a private bus company began operation of express service on the nine-mile portion on the East-West Freeway of Milwaukee. Since that time, four more routes have been added for the same type of operation. The five routes now serve over 2,200 passengers who would have brought over 1,500 automobiles into the city if the freeway express bus service was not present.[17]

In order to ascertain whether the Freeway Flyer patrons had been simply diverted from the regular bus service or automobile commuters, a careful survey was conducted two weeks after the inauguration of the service in 1964. This survey confirmed that the Freeway Flyer service had indeed attracted many new transit patrons, most of whom had previously been automobile commuters.[18] Of a total of 187 respondents, 73 persons had formerly commuted by a mode other than bus, and 54 of these were former auto commuters. It is significant that only 29 respondents were captive transit riders in that they had no driver's licenses. Furthermore, survey results showed that 66 percent of the respondents did own an automobile which was available for commuting if they had chosen to drive.[19] A similar survey was repeated in 1966 after the Bayshore route had been added. By this time, the number of commuters converting to transit service at Mayfair had increased from 73 in 1964 to 227 in 1966.[20] Those who converted to transit—again mostly auto drivers—now represented more than 51 percent of the total patronage as compared to 39 percent in 1964. Those who converted to transit on the Bayshore run accounted for 58 percent of total ridership. Nearly two-thirds of the respondents on both routes said that they commuted by transit out of choice and one-third of the respondents said they could not have driven because an automobile was not available at the time of the trip. Less than 5 percent of those surveyed at both routes did not own automobiles.

Between 80 and 90 percent of the passengers on the Freeway Flyer service were travelers between home and work. It was also found that 84 percent of the points of origin and destinations of the Mayfair passengers in 1964 (which changed to 74 percent in 1966) were located within three miles of the line terminus at the shopping center; another 21 percent (18 percent in 1966) within three to six miles, and 5 percent (8 percent in 1966) beyond six miles. On the Bayshore route in 1966, 69 percent of the origins and destinations were located within three miles of the terminus at the shopping center; 21 percent within three to six miles and 10 percent beyond six miles.

Ridership on the Mayfair Shopping Center-Downtown Milwaukee route increased steadily from 290 passengers per workday during the first month of service to 600 by the end of the first year, and by January 1967 was approaching 1,000 passengers. In 1965, a similar service was initiated on a new route from the Bayshore Shopping Center, located in Glendale six miles north of downtown Milwaukee. Patronage at Bayshore had by 1966 approximately doubled the daily average recorded during the first month of operation.

The success of the express bus service is attributable to a great degree to the availability of free parking space in parking lots of outlying shopping centers. A survey revealed that 45 percent of respondents at Mayfair and 49 percent at Bayshore drove to the shopping center to catch buses; 29 percent and 34 percent, respectively, arrived as auto passengers; 16 percent and 15 percent walked; and 5 percent and 9 percent took buses and transferred. Now, because the East-West Freeway is already so heavily loaded in rush periods, Milwaukee County is considering the establishment of a separate bus right of way, paralleling the present East-West Freeway.

1. *User benefits*

Time Savings. On reaching the downtown area, the express buses operate over a limited downtown loop, providing patrons with a faster and cheaper mode of transportation that reaches closer to their work locations.

Buses operated on the Mayfair and downtown Milwaukee routes reduced the travel time over regular bus service on surface arteries from 56 to 33 minutes, a reduction of 41 percent. Similarly, the Freeway Flyer service on the Bayshore run saved commuters as much as 23 minutes, compared to the regular bus service travel times of 49 minutes, despite the fact that one intermediate stop was made at an intersection a few blocks from the shopping center.[21]

Monetary savings. Patrons who drive to the bus are offered free parking as well as a reasonable premium fare which, including one hour's free transfer time to other lines, is only five cents higher than the regular bus fare of 30 cents.[22]

2. *Community benefits.* According to survey results, 26 percent of the respondents at Mayfair and 31 percent at Bayshore indicated that the frequency of their shopping trips had increased slightly, and 19 percent and 17 percent, respectively, indicated a considerable increase in their patronage of the respective shopping centers.[23]

The City of Milwaukee estimated that each private automobile registered costs the taxpayer $70.12 annually (average from 1962 through 1966).[24] Further, the deficit between highway-related expenditures and highway-related revenues (license fees, gasoline taxes, and other motor vehicle imposts) amounted to $16,736,377, primarily covered by real estate taxes. This amount constitutes 17.2 percent of the annual total city costs covered by real estate and other taxes to provide all city government services. Thus, conversion of private automobile commuters to public transit is seen by the city as a means to lower not only highway and street congestion but also the burden on the city's tax monies.

The Metro Flyer Express Bus

The one-year project bus service in Baltimore City, Maryland, was to test the practicability of providing a suburban, low-density, high-income residential area with express bus service to downtown Baltimore employment, shopping, and recreational centers. The modern, air-conditioned express bus system serviced the 19,000 residents of Towson and its several adjoining suburban areas of Maryland.

During the project period, passenger usage increased by 193 percent after one month of operation, and by the close of the project the Metro Flyer was carrying 496 riders a day. The route took limited access highways for approximately 72 percent of the one-way trip. At the end of the project in April 1967, the service was continued by the private carrier with minor modifications; actually the experiment had constituted an expansion of the existing local service with the same operator providing the service. The estimated cost of the project was $80,025, of which 53,350 was federally financed.[25]

For many Metro Flyer patrons, the route was within walking distance of their homes, while for others the free parking facilities permitted economical use of their automobiles. Moreover, the air-conditioned modern buses provided fast, comfortable, and economical travel to the downtown commuter destination. The passenger distribution routing within the central business district delivered passengers within walking distance of their final destinations. More than half of the patrons surveyed had not been transit riders prior to the project service.

The Metro Flyer, now incorporated into the operator's transit system, has been a profitable operation. Although, according to a survey, 26.8 percent of the passengers had shifted to the Flyer from the existing local transit service, this was not detrimental to the total transit operation. In fact, the passenger shift provided room on local buses for expanding patronage without increasing the local service requirements.

Capital Flyer Express Bus Project

The two-way express bus demonstration project linked central Washington, D.C., to the Maryland suburbs of Prince George's and Montgomery Counties and the Virginia suburb of Fairfax County. The objective was twofold. First, as a potential means of tackling the rising peak-period highway congestion by car commuters, the project offered suburban communities modern express transit service to downtown Washington and free parking facilities, and second, to provide inner-city residents access to suburban job opportunities, the project ran preferentially reduced-fare direct bus service.

The D.C. Transit System, Inc. was contracted for service between Washington, D.C., and the Maryland suburbs; and the Washington, Virginia and Maryland Coach Company, Inc. was contracted for the lines between Washington, D.C., and the Virginia suburbs. Daytime parking was provided free to suburban commuters at the parking facilities of several Virginia and Maryland shopping centers.

The express bus service providing inner-city residents access to their potential jobs in the suburbs was supplemented by efforts to recruit manpower in the District and to identify employment opportunities along the Capital Flyer routes. In this endeavor, assistance was sought from a number of Washington, D.C., manpower agencies.

Project bus service operated to each of the three counties for a period of 18 months. The project operator, the Metropolitan Washington Council of Governments, hoped to see the private bus companies carrying out the subsidized operations to absorb the Capital Flyer lines into their own networks as permanent links. An indication of the program's success is the fact that most Capital Flyer routes were taken over by the bus companies, although sometimes with modifications in the frequency of service.

Ridership began at a low level, but, as the project time and experience accumulated, large increases in ridership were observed. The highest passenger volume for the entire system was reached in November 1970, when an average of 1,419 passengers per day rode the buses. A total of 463,343 riders used the Capital Flyer service during the project period, 320,167 as commuters and 143,176 as reverse commuters.[26]

Summary

Express bus service programs have been instituted for the purpose of providing efficient commuter transportation between suburban communities and the central city area. Free parking facilities are provided at the suburban terminus, which is located at a shopping center, and this constitutes a major inducer for automobile commuters to switch to the bus mode.

In the three cases of express commuter bus service cited above—the "Freeway Flyer" of Milwaukee, "Capital Flyer" of Washington, D.C., and "Metro Flyer" of Baltimore—all realized significant success in attracting ridership. New, comfortable bus equipment is providing former driver commuters or former users of less reliable, less direct public transportation with a faster, cheaper, and more pleasant daily trip to their jobs.

In addition, the former auto commuters are now provided with opportunities to save parking costs that might be required if they drove into the center city area. Furthermore, the owning of the commuter car which is unused all day if brought to the city, could be used by other members of the household and perhaps reduce the number of second and/or third family cars.

The diversion of automobile drivers to the bus leaves the highway less congested, thereby allowing faster flow for the rest of the city-bound commuters. The automobiles that are no longer brought into the congested core-city means fewer sources of air and noise pollution.

Many of the inner-city residents are poor, as well as unemployed or underemployed, but their lack of mobility seriously hampers their attempts to reach jobs in suburban locations. One of the programs—the Capital Flyer program—was designed to provide transport links for the inner-city residents to reach these suburban job opportunities on the reverse trip after discharging inbound commuters in Washington, D.C., center.

Finally, the shopping centers which provide free parking spaces for the commuters are being rewarded with patronage from the bus riders.

New Equipment

General

The American Transit Association (ATA) estimated that in 1971, over 43 percent of the 50,000 transit buses in operation were over 10 years old.[27] Since two-thirds of the transit passengers are carried by bus, a large number of transit users are being served by outdated, inefficient buses. The air pollutants emitted by these buses are also a serious problem.

In the following pages, descriptions are given of specific examples of new equipment purchases made possible through UMTA grants. Oftentimes, acquisitions of new equipment for replacing or upgrading the used fleet constitute only part of a series of comprehensive efforts to sustain or improve the bus transit as it exists. These efforts may include a public body's taking over a failing private operation, incorporation of progressive management approaches to better respond to demand or various specific measures for improving the quality of service through additions of service area routes covered, and increasing frequency and reliability of service. Instances of improved quality of transit service are discussed in the next section.

Sumter, South Carolina

In 1970, the City of Sumter, South Carolina, was awarded a grant (SC-UTG-1) for the purchase of four new 35-passenger, air-conditioned diesel transit buses.

Since 1960, ridership on Sumter's B & H Bus Lines has remained at low— although relatively stable—levels.[28] The line's revenues in 1960 amounted to $54,601.07, which increased slightly by 1968 to $57,569.40. Today's riders are largely made up of low-income people, children, the aged, and the physically infirm. For these people, B & H buses represent the sole means of urban transportation.

In recent years, two new industries have located in the Sumter community, both providing over 1,000 unskilled jobs. At present, no buses or any other form of public transportation serve the area, and the proposed enlargement of the bus system would serve many of these workers.

Sumter is also planning to construct 200 low-rent public housing units. Since the relocation resources prevented the city from using urban renewal to clear areas, however, these units will be constructed on sites which are removed from all the present bus line routes. Thus, an expanded bus system with new equipment would serve these housing sites.

Alameda-Contra Costa, California

During 1972 Alameda-Contra Costa Transit District was awarded a grant (CAL-UTG-42) to be used toward the purchase of 215 new buses.

The Alameda-Contra Costa Transit operates 699 buses over approximately 1,270 route miles. Of these buses, 462 are of the "new look" type, which have been acquired since 1961. Its ridership has shown a steady increase from

47,816,000 riders in 1961 to 52,378,000 in 1969.[29] This growth is attributable to improvements in equipment and services, extensions of lines, and vigorous promotion and advertising. Further, the transit system has exerted efforts to accommodate the special needs of the elderly and handicapped by furnishing special stanchions and safety flooring in the new buses.

Wilmington, Delaware (DEL-UTG-1)

The Delaware Authority for Regional Transit (DART) purchased 55 new 45-passenger air-conditioned diesel transit buses in 1971 and had selected sites for construction of its new garage building and operating headquarters as of June 30, 1971. Also the purchase of 81 locked fare boxes was being negotiated.

Wilmington has close to four million annual riders who are dependent on public transportation, many of whom are children, the elderly, and the poor. While regular route service has been maintained at the levels scheduled in May 1970, the new equipment led to an increase of service equivalent to an additional 10,514 miles and 877 hours per week.[30]

Early in 1971, increases in patronage became apparent. This favorable trend is attributable to improvements in the bus service made possible by the new equipment and to the route extensions, as well as to active public promotion subsequent to the change of name from Greater Wilmington Transportation Authority to DART. The campaign, inaugurated in May 1971, has helped to change the negative public image of the bus company to a more positive one and has helped to win the public's support. In addition, a loop service to the Model Cities area was begun in October 1970, and a campaign to promote the Authority's new express schedule has further enhanced its image as a promoter of public transportation.

Along with the acute scarcity of parking space for commuters and shoppers, air pollution is among the most serious problems faced by the city. Wilmington is reported to suffer from the third highest saturation of pollutants, such as dust, smoke, and droplets, among 200 localities tested by the U.S. Public Health Service.[31] Consequently, the engine in the new equipment is designed to reduce pollution and smoke through a device called a low sac needle—for achieving greater combustion efficiency—and catalytic muffler, according to a General Motors report cited in the *Passenger Transport.*

Washington, D.C.

Washington, D.C., requested assistance to purchase 15 medium-sized buses for operation of a feeder-distributor service within the central employment area (CEA).[32]

1. *User benefits.* The CEA (primarily composed of the downtown, the southwest, and lower Connecticut Avenue) has the largest concentration of jobs in the Washington metropolitan region—286,302, or roughly one-third of the region's total.[33] A forecast estimates this number to increase to 327,013 by 1976.

The medium-sized buses for performing the feeder-distribution service—which partially incorporates the Dial-A-Ride concept—are estimated to serve potential employee ridership of 97,142 passengers a day. This size may be expected to increase to 153,631 by 1976.[34] In addition, the internal circulation service during off-peak hours would improve the availability of public transit for a substantial number of potential riders. Presently, the minibus service within the downtown retail core only (along F, 7th, and 8th Streets, N.W.) carries 3,100 passengers a day. Based on the similar relationship of this ridership to the number of employees working in the immediate service area, an improved and extended internal circulation service to be offered by the medium-size buses may serve more than 5,800 riders and by 1976 more than 6,600 riders.[35]

2. *Operator benefits.* At present, the four transit companies operating line-haul buses during peak hours in this area must terminate, originate, or pass through the CEA. Consequently, this intensely used, highly developed, and congested area consumes a substantial part of the time required to complete the line-haul runs. Thus, the transit companies are forced to maintain a large fleet of line-haul buses to provide adequate services, despite the fact that many of the buses are not fully utilized during the off-peak hours. The acquisition of medium-size buses to serve a feeder-distributor function within the CEA would free a good number of line-haul buses to be recirculated quickly during the peak periods. This arrangement would significantly increase economy and efficiency of the transit companies, as well as the overall transit service they provide. Easily maneuverable medium-size vehicles, equipped with appropriate braking, fuel, and other systems for serving the congested area, would also substantially reduce operating and maintenance costs.

3. *Community benefits.* Among the benefits to accrue from the use of medium-size buses will be reduced traffic congestion within the CEA. The proposed buses with special equipment would result in less air and noise pollution. Moreover, an improved and expanded internal circulation system would help toward revitalizing the downtown area, commensurate with various environmental improvement plans being worked out for this area, such as the creation of predominantly pedestrian areas.

Hato Rey, Commonwealth of Puerto Rico

The Metropolitan Bus Authority of Hato Rey, Puerto Rico, was awarded a grant toward the purchase of 50 new 45-passenger, air-conditioned diesel transit buses for serving the urban area of San Juan (August 25, 1971, PR-UTG-9).

1. *User benefits.* Compared to the number of passengers carried in Fiscal Year 1958-1959 (58,771,862 passengers), the number in Fiscal Year 1969-1970 registered a slight drop (58,038,838 passengers). However, as shown in Table 5-2, there had been consistently healthy annual increases until 1969-1970.

The recent drop in ridership is attributable to a lack of buses to service the demand. In 1968-69, the average number of buses on the street during peak hours was 290, declining to 260 buses in 1969-70.[36] Due to the shortage of buses, the Metropolitan Bus Authority was operating about two-thirds to three-fourths of scheduled service on most of its major lines.

Dependency on public transportation by the San Juan public is substantially higher than in comparable U.S. cities. Approximately 37 percent of the average weekday trips in the San Juan Metropolitan Area are made on public transportation systems, largely due to the low level of car ownership. For example, according to 1964 figures, almost 50 percent of the San Juan area households did not own a car, while only 10 percent had more than one car. Further, a good portion of the public bus riders are school children (numbering 1,112,579 in 1969-1970), because the Commonwealth Department of Education does not provide for any transportation in the operation of its school systems. Instead, it contributes one-half the cost of the children's fares to the bus operator.

2. *Operator benefits.* The new buses are expected to bring a reduction of approximately $400,000 a year in maintenance costs.[37]

Table 5-2
Number of Passengers and Miles Served

FY	Passengers	Miles
1958-59	58,771,862	11,071,521
1959-60	60,342,198	11,248,388
1960-61	63,001,006	11,780,637
1961-62	64,982,281	11,948,953
1962-63	65,870,704	12,884,991
1963-64	66,634,724	13,298,071
1964-65	62,496,249	13,001,355
1965-66	65,602,022	13,710,006
1966-67	66,398,065	13,698,494
1967-68	66,090,941	13,947,445
1968-69	65,751,815	14,437,776
1969-70	58,038,838	13,062,218

Source: U.S. Department of Transportation, UMTA, Approval Memo for Capital Grant Project PR-UTG-9, Dated August 25, 1971.

Providence, Rhode Island

In 1969, due to the success of an earlier capital grant project, the Rhode Island Public Transit Authority requested capital grant assistance for the purchase of 45 new transit buses to replace antiquated vehicles (17 years or older).

Bus service was increased in 1966 for the first time since the 1950s. This was accompanied by a sufficient increase in revenue passengers for the system to show a slight operating profit for the years 1966 through 1968 without resorting to a fare increase. The ridership increase is primarily attributed to the 102 new buses put into service in 1966.[38] The purchase of these buses was financed in part through a UMTA grant RI-UTG-1.

Other Examples of New Equipment

1. *Savannah, Georgia.* The transit system in Savannah became a municipal operation several years ago with the main objective of maintaining a constant passenger level. The records of 1968 through 1970 show that this objective is being achieved, and the reason for this successful attempt is being attributed primarily to its consistent attempt to maintain the quality and quantity of its equipment.

2. *Erie, Pennsylvania.* In Erie, a transit authority took over the transit system which had been losing passengers at a rapid rate until several years ago. In 1970, the system realized a 10 percent growth in passenger level over the constant level of the previous two years. The operator's attempts to modernize the fleet have been instrumental in achieving this growth. The former run-down buses were replaced by a fleet of 50 new buses, which was later supplemented by five more through a separate grant. A new garage was constructed to house these buses.

3. *Long Beach, California.* Long Beach is typical of many other California communities where transit is generally hard to operate efficiently due to a dispersed pattern of development. However, the city has been experiencing a startling increase in ridership over the past several years, and the well-maintained fleet of buses has played a major part in achieving this increase.

4. *San Diego, California.* A municipal corporation was formed several years ago to acquire a transit system serving the large low-density city of San Diego. The system had been experiencing steadily decreasing passenger levels. Upgrading the fleet of buses has been a major policy under the new management, and 100 new air-conditioned diesel transit coaches were purchased. As a consequence, an increase in ridership of 6.5 percent was recorded in 1969 over the previous year.

5. *Lafayette, Louisiana.* The transit operation of this small city in northwestern Louisiana had been acquired by the county from private operators. Partly due to a fleet of new air-conditioned buses, its ridership increased by 4.6 percent in 1969 and by 4.7 percent in 1970.

6. *Trenton, New Jersey.* Subsequent to the public ownership of a local transit company, funds were provided for the purchase of 20 new buses, bus shelters, signs, and building rehabilitation. As of April 1971, the project was about 80 percent completed. Although it is too early to predict the level of the project's success, the new buses on the street are expected to enhance the public image of a local transit operation to an important degree.

7. *Battle Creek, Michigan.* A city-owned bus company serves this small community exclusively with the 17 small buses funded under MICH-UTG-9. The grant of $138,500 (approved in October 1969) financed the purchase of these buses along with miscellaneous supporting equipment including bus washers. These new buses are small and compact and are ideally suited to maintain the small amount of transit traffic which exists in this type of small community.

Summary

The run-down equipment presently employed in many of the nation's cities has been responsible for having caused the public to associate an unattractive image with many of the transit bus services. Even those captive riders who have little choice but to depend on public transportation have come to avoid riding the bus, often forcing them to resort to purchasing automobiles or other means of transit. Consequently, upgrading the quality of equipment for the existing and expected service constitutes the basic aspect for providing reliable, inexpensive, fast transit. In some cases, as exemplified by the experience of San Juan, the service level had to be cut due to lack of enough equipment.

As shown by the specific examples cited here, however, acquisition of new buses, in conjunction with new service coverage and new management approaches, have resulted in instant increases in ridership. As in Sumter, S.C., the newly created demand by captive riders through new industry and public housing projects in areas previously uncovered by transit would have had to remain unmet without additional buses. Part of the new fleet acquired for Alameda-Contra Costa Counties was directed toward accommodating the special needs of the elderly and handicapped through extra equipment features and safety considerations. Thus, new, attractive, comfortable buses not only induce people to use transit—resulting in badly needed revenue increases—but also increase operating efficiency for transit operators.

Further, new buses featuring up-to-date engine combustion efficiency are a welcome development for many cities whose air pollution and noise level have reached an alarming state, as shown by the example of Wilmington.

Attracting a greater number of travelers to bus transit further results in decreasing cities' urgent needs for more parking spaces in the prime center-city locations. Also, as in Washington, D.C., the addition of new medium-sized buses on the streets of the central employment area frees line-haul buses from the time-consuming drives in this congested region. The smaller buses adopted for a feeder-distributor and internal circulation function were anticipated to result in more convenient transit service for both commuters and shoppers, and the improved circulation of the central area is anticipated to produce a positive effect on the general revitalization of the city's downtown area.

Quality of Service

General

Antiquated equipment, rising labor costs, increased vandalism and crime rates, and declining patronage due to competition from private automobiles have taken their toll on transit operations. Over the last 15 years, 131 cities throughout the United States have had transit services discontinued.[39] For example, a study conducted by Voorhees in Honolulu indicated several inadequacies in the quality of bus transit service which make the aged systems unable to attract new patronage.[40] These include the following:

1. High load factors—standees are common even during off-peak hours.
2. Low scheduled reliability, particularly during peak hours during which traffic congestion is a major factor.
3. No interservice transfer—full fare is necessary.
4. Unserved and poorly served areas due to lack of service or poor orientation of routes.
5. Excessive travel time—5 to 15 percent of riders served by transit require more than an hour and a half to reach a major center by bus.
6. Aged buses—average age of transit buses is 15 years, and they lack attractiveness and comfort.
7. Lack of special equipment—buses used to transport school children have no rear doors.
8. Inadequate information services—no specific schedules are available for the buses.

Several UMTA capital grants have made a significant contribution toward improving the quality of transit system service in an attempt to reverse the trend of declining patronage, and indirectly assisting in the maintenance of transit systems that would otherwise have disappeared.

Quality of transit service encompasses the following major aspects:

1. Establishment of new and expanded service.
2. Reduction in fares.

3. Increase in frequency and reliability of service.
4. Extension of scheduled service hours.
5. Upgrading of fleet.
6. Intermodal integration of service.

Since the last two categories are discussed in separate sections of this study, the following pages will list specific examples relating to the first four quality-of-service topics.

Erie, Pennsylvania

Until several years ago the city had been served by a private company (Erie Coach Co.) which was unable to maintain adequate transit service and which experienced rapidly declining ridership. An UMTA grant assisted a new transit authority, the Erie Metropolitan Transportation Authority, to take over the system. A grant of $1.6 million was approved in August 1967 (PA-UTG-5).[41]

Upon recommendation of a study financed by a grant of $16,000, new routes were added and a large-scale marketing program was initiated to publicize the many passenger amenities that had been added. After two years, which saw the passenger level maintained at a constant level, a 10 percent increase was registered by 1970.

San Diego, California

With federal assistance, the City of San Diego acquired the assets of the San Diego Transit System (CAL-UTG-12). Since the change of ownership, the following improvements have been accomplished.

1. An extension of route miles from 302.92 to 332.94.
2. An improved frequency of service on all 23 routes.
3. Reduced fares from $1.10 for four rides to $1.00, and reduced student fares from 25 cents to 20 cents.
4. Initiation of a senior citizen fare of 20 cents for first two zones.
5. Initiation of a special 50-cent fare to San Diego Stadium from any place on the system.
6. Initiation of a Sunday and holiday fare of 75 cents good for all day on the entire system.

As a result, annual ridership increased from 15,111,419 passengers in 1967 to 17,130,808 in 1968.[42] Despite fare reductions, revenue for the fiscal year ending June 30, 1968, increased by 1.6 percent,[43] and employment increased by 11 percent with the addition of 446 new bus drivers. (See section on new equipment in this chapter.)

Other Examples

In Lafayette, Louisiana the transit system run by private operators has recently been purchased by the county. Based upon recommendations resulting from a careful study, numerous route changes and a general increase in service were initiated, and a significant increase in ridership has been attained. A similar situation was experienced in Trenton, New Jersey, after the Mercer County Improvement Authority was established in 1968 to save and upgrade service previously handled by a financially destitute private transit company.

Summary

If the nation's bus transit is not only to survive from operators' financial standpoint, but to provide adequate services from the riders' standpoint, the quality of service must receive utmost attention. If acceptable quality is available, more travelers will patronize bus transit in order to be relieved of both tedious driving on congested highways in peak hours and costly automobile operating, parking, or ownership expenditures. Also, convenient, reliable, and inexpensive bus transit can well serve those travelers without an automobile or those unable to drive, in areas where rapid transit is not present or is currently infeasible.

In various cities of the nation, UMTA-financed resources have assisted in revitalizing bus services through increased ridership by offering improved service, such as expansion of coverage areas or scheduled hours, increased frequency and reliability, reduction in fares, and improved equipment quality.

The examples of Trenton, New Jersey; Erie, Pennsylvania; Lafayette, Louisiana; and San Diego, California, cited above represent only a few of those across the country which are exerting efforts to revitalize the bus transit through attention to quality of service. Such bus service is instrumental in achieving equality of mobility for a greater number of people for reaching jobs and other opportunities.

Overburdened peak-period highways and city streets can be made less congested as more automobile drivers switch to bus transit, thus resulting in improved traffic flow for all vehicles. Likewise, a reduction in the number of cars on city streets in the downtown area requires less available parking space and results in applying the prime space more efficiently. Improved circulation on city streets also makes the downtown area more attractive for shoppers.

6 Commuter Rail

The Skokie Swift

General

The Skokie Swift is a rail rapid transit commuter service that shuttles from Skokie, Illinois, a suburb north of Chicago, to a rapid transit terminal at the Chicago city limits. The distance of five miles is traveled in six and one-half minutes with no stops. Service is provided between 6 A.M. and 11 P.M. on weekdays, at headways during rush hours of three to four minutes. Weekend service is less frequent. The one-way fare of 50 cents includes a free transfer to the city rapid system on which the basic fare is 30 cents.

Passengers residing outside Chicago come primarily from Skokie and nearby Morton Grove, with 25 percent from other communities. Their destinations are dispersed within four square miles of the central city. Over 25 percent of all passengers are residents of the Chicago central city who travel in reverse to suburban jobs. Current daily volume totals 7,500 to 8,000 passengers. A parking facility at the Skokie station accommodates 555 cars and offers separate areas for loading and unloading riders from autos and feeder buses. The daily parking rate is 25 cents. Coordination was established with feeder bus operators as well as CTA facilities at the Chicago city limits.

The Skokie Swift originated as a two-year public transit demonstration project (April 1964-1966) in which the Village of Skokie and the CTA obtained partial financing from the Housing and Home Finance Agency to rehabilitate an unused right of way and equipment, and to operate weekday service for ridership anticipated at 1,600 passengers daily after two years. As soon as service began in April 1964, actual ridership exceeded planned estimates by three to four times. Intensive advertising and promotion is credited with stimulating the sizable immediate ridership (20 percent of the planned first-year revenues were to be spent on advertising). Satisfaction with the speed, reliability, and convenience of the service led to permanent ridership.

In the second year of the project, 3,500,000 riders were served, and in more recent years this figure has risen to over 4,000,000, five times original expectations. After the demonstration phase, the CTA took over the Skokie Swift operations, sought HUD financing for further improvements, and now runs the extension as part of its total rapid transit network. The line has generated considerably more revenue per car mile for the same operating cost than other rapid transit segments; its sponsors believe its success has demonstrated that "motorists can be lured from their autos when high speed mass transit is provided," to quote George S. DeMent,[1] CTA Board Chairman in 1966, and that public transit is feasible and economically justifiable for daily peak ridership volumes well below the 10,000 to 40,000 bench mark used by many rail transit planners.[2]

Need for the Service

In defining objectives for the Skokie Swift Demonstration Project, its sponsors stated that they sought to (i) determine the effectiveness and economic feasibility of linking a fast-growing, medium density suburban area with a central city by means of a high-speed rail rapid transit extension coordinated with suburban buses and with the central city's extensive transit network; and (ii) develop thorough surveys and studies useful guidelines for public officials and planners on whether a similar type of service should or can be provided in other large metropolitan areas.

Skokie area residents lacked rapid rail service as an alternative for reaching the central city system, even though a right of way existed where two rail services had operated over a 40-year period. Each had eventually failed—the first, with nine stops over the five-mile route, ended in 1948; and the other, an interurban electric service, ended in 1961. Residents of Skokie (then a village of 68,000) tried to finance reorganization of the rail service but failed. The CTA agreed to take over operations if rehabilitation could be financed. It invested $1.700 million to acquire the right of way, then together with Skokie obtained $349,217 of federal funds to augment its own commitment of $137,415 and Skokie's of $37,193 to undertake operations for a two-year period. The Skokie contribution was for parking lot construction and maintenance, a promotional campaign, and before-and-after studies to measure changes in land use, property value, traffic patterns, and vacancy sales. Federal funds supplied the necessary financing for right of way and equipment rehabilitation.

Benefits of the Services

1. *User benefits.* The Skokie Swift filled a definite gap in the range of transportation choices available to Skokie and Chicago residents by providing a service that met current expectations and standards for speed, convenience, and reliability. Specifically, it:

a. Provided a substantial daily ridership with a transportation choice that equaled or exceeded the speed and convenience of their current mode at a reasonable cost. (The five-mile trip required six and one-half minutes plus loading and unloading time, contrasted with at least 15 minutes by car in rush hour conditions and longer by bus.)

b. Provided automobile drivers and passengers with the option of using mass transit by establishing convenient parking and "Kiss-'N'-Ride" areas. (One-third of all riders park; one-third use "Kiss-'N'-Ride"; the remaining one-third use the bus.)

c. Opened job opportunities in suburban Skokie and vicinity to central city residents who did not own automobiles and thereby effectively lacked access to the suburbs because existing alternatives required up to two hours' travel time each way. Also, it permitted these residents to remain in lower cost urban housing and find employment in the expanding suburban labor market.

d. Represented feasible transportation to about 30 percent of the riders who formerly did not make trips between Skokie and Chicago by any mode.

e. Permitted a more dispersed population to have easy access to public transit by establishing coordinated feeder bus routes.

f. Provided better quality service than was provided by bus service over a similar route to the city limit terminal, both in speed and frequency interval.

2. *Operator benefits.* In the period immediately before Skokie Swift service began, no rail service was operating along the Skokie-Chicago right of way. A bus service roughly paralleled the right of way, and the Eden and Kennedy expressways carried auto traffic, while other commuters used rail service originating in other suburbs.

As operator, the CTA has experienced:

a. Capture of new riders for city public transit who formerly traveled entirely by auto, rail, or bus (40 percent of Skokie riders).

b. Capture of an additional segment of total trip for auto and bus riders who formerly did not enter CTA until Chicago city limits.

c. Capture of new riders who formerly did not make either the primary trip (suburban residents) or the reverse trip (city residents) at all (30 percent of riders).

d. Earnings per car mile that were double the normal rate for the city despite similar operating costs per car mile.

e. Fivefold increase in productivity over prior operator. (Compared to the last year of electric railroad operations by the Chicago, North Shore, and Milwaukee line on this route, when 1,600 riders were using the right of way, the new ridership of 7,000 to 8,000 represents a fivefold increase in productivity.)

f. Complementary gains to bus ridership. Bus operators experienced a short-term decline in the ridership on the route parallel to the right of way, but this change was more than offset by increased passengers using the lines as feeders to the Skokie Swift.

g. Enhanced reputation and experience which assisted in later implementation of plans to use the median strip of two expressways as the rights of way for additional CTA public transit extensions.

3. *Community benefits*. The Skokie Swift has:

a. Developed for the community a reputation for pragmatic leadership in implementing a service whose success contrasted with traditional doubts regarding the feasibility of such a line.

b. Created a model for similar services in Chicago or other large metropolitan areas. (Extensions of the CTA system along the Kennedy and Dan Ryan Expressways in Chicago have profited from the Skokie experience regarding necessary conveniences.)

c. Opened up a flow of new labor from the central city to fill jobs in suburban commerce and industry. Four types of workers—nonwhite, women, skilled blue-collar, and unskilled workers—became available to local employers as a result of the Skokie Swift.

d. Improved employee stability for the firms located near it. Both the new-hires rate and the quit rate for these firms were substantially below that of firms with access only to other transit or to no transit at all.

e. Provided a transit extension with a public investment that represented substantial savings through rehabilitation and use of an existing right of way rather than undertaking new construction.

f. Demonstrated the need for public investment to recondition a right of way, equipment, and facilities in order to open up an acceptable quality of mass commuter service.

g. Demonstrated that it is unnecessary under certain conditions to run long trains with multiple stops and to supply direct through service from the suburbs to the central city itself (rather than to the city's mass transit system).

h. Supplied evidence that many motorists will switch to mass transit if they can get a time-saving, reliable, and convenient service. (Traffic counts produced inconclusive evidence about a possible reduction in auto movement onto the nearby expressway, but 20 percent of riders did indicate they had formerly used automobiles. A park-and-ride facility with access from highways is essential at an outlying terminal in order to service transit riders being fed by autos.

i. Improved apartment rental market. (While not directly measured, the reference to the Skokie Swift service in apartment rental ads assisted in placing the rentals and in contributing to a continued annual 5 percent rise in apartment rent levels. In addition, new apartment construction was attributed to the proximity of the service.)

j. Developed recognition and community pride among residents. (96 percent of a 520-household sample could identify the label "Skokie Swift," and 82 percent of these considered the service a very important contribution to the community. Only 1.2 percent did not find it important at all.)

k. Developed a good transit image for the community.

Summary

The Skokie Swift represents one of the best examples in the country of the success which a well-planned and well-run commuter service can attain. Most important, it has demonstrated the value of commuter rail service in diverting traffic away from other overcrowded modes, especially the highway. The Skokie Swift, in many ways, has become a model for other lines, such as the Lindenwold line running from Philadelphia to Lindenwold, N.J., of how a publicly subsidized investment in commuter-rail marketing concepts can pay handsome rewards in terms of community and operator benefits.

Different from rapid transit, the Skokie Swift commuter line is longer and has relatively fewer stops; therefore, it requires less power for rapid acceleration and stopping but nevertheless can reach very high speeds. Thus, it has provided a solution to the regional transportation needs of a Chicago suburb. Its benefits include the opportunity for expansion into yet undeveloped suburban land areas for new residential growth. Because of its nonstop six and one-half minute run to downtown rapid transit facilities, 30 percent of the total ridership is composed of 2,400 new commuters who found it feasible to live in and commute from Skokie.

Other benefits of the Skokie Swift include an appreciation of real estate values in Skokie, travel cost savings, a fivefold increase in fare-box results over the previous operator, improved revenue per mile of operation as compared with other CTA lines, and better employment mobility. The related benefits not discussed above were provision of better airport access, better accessibility for travelers from outside the community, and improved service for the poor, elderly, and youth. These were not relevant to the objectives of the Skokie Swift line, which are to provide a better service to suburban commuters and to help relieve congestion in other modes of transportation.

The Philadelphia Lindenwold Line

General

In many ways the history of Philadelphia rail transportation tells the story of the general decline of rapid transit in the late 50s and early 60s. Philadelphia's suburban communities stretch out from the Center City along several major lines of the Reading and Penn-Central Railroads. The Reading Railroad's northeast extension runs toward Levittown and Trenton, New Jersey, in the northeast; the Penn-Central and the Reading operate lines through Germantown and Chestnut Hill to the northwest; and Paoli and the "mainline" communities to the west are served by the Penn-Central as are Media and Westchester to the southwest, and Chester and Wilmington to the south.

Because of this rail structure, Greater Philadelphia's transportation network has always been oriented toward rail commuter operations. Typically, then, until the early 60s, the commuter services as well as the Philadelphia Transit Authority's (PTC) subway and trolley lines had been run by the old railroad school belief that handling people was not much different from hauling freight, and that it was not a social service but a profit-making venture. Consequently, as operating costs—largely wages—began to bite, the general reaction of transit and commuter rail management was to cut costs and raise fares. As this syndrome began to repeat itself, a sadly ancient and deteriorated transit system evolved.[3] As a result of this, the railroads and transit lines began losing passengers in the late 50s just when the highway boom was gaining momentum. This timing accentuated the downward financial spiral until 1962 when the PTC finally went into receivership.

It was largely at this time that public concern began to mount about the future of rail transit in Philadelphia. For one thing, two new major arteries leading into the city had been built or were under construction, and the most notable of them—the Schuylkill Expressway—was already grossly inadequate to handle the burgeoning auto commuter traffic from northwest Philadelphia. Because of terrain and heavy industrial concentrations, regional planners began to realize there was a limit to the number of highway lanes that would be built downtown. Furthermore, they determined that traffic had reached a point in 1962 where each commuter auto was costing the city $170 per year in highway, traffic, and police costs. It was at that time that planners and the public in general began to view rail transit as an indispensable public service which, even if run by a public authority at a deficit that taxpayers would have to subsidize, was worth it. They also suddenly realized that the best way to run a rail service from a patronage viewpoint was not from a defensive, cost sensitive posture that obviously had debilitating effects on riders. This realization largely resulted from the fact that even though studies showed an overwhelming demand for transit facilities, rail transit was losing more people each year. At the same time they discovered that consumers actually had a set of definite preferences—aside from cost—for the mode of transportation they rode which, if understood, could be used to entice them back onto the rail lines. Thus, marketing principles were discovered by Philadelphia transit planners, and, as a first crack at rejuvenating ridership, the "Philadelphia plan" was put into action.

Very simply, the Philadelphia plan was a joint effort on the part of the city and the Reading and Penn-Central Railroads to improve the level of service to a point where commuters would leave their cars at home and begin taking the train again. Fares were chopped in half, and the frequency of service was increased to a level that made it extremely convenient for shoppers as well as commuters. Service improvements were first introduced on two lines to northeast Philadelphia, one operated by the Pennsylvania Railroad and one by the Reading Railroad. Both lines cut fares to a flat 30 cents—about half of the former cost. They also added more trains and, for an extra dime, offered a transfer on PTC buses and trolleys. At the same time the city organized the Passenger Service Improvement Corporation (PSIC) to manage all six Philadelphia suburban railroad operations. The people of Philadelphia also subsidized the Reading and Pennsylvania Railroads in an amount to equal all their excess losses over previous losses. About a year later the PSIC did the same thing for the Reading Railroad's northeast line to Fox Chase—Operation Northeast. The results of the PSIC's programs were dramatic. By 1964, on the two lines of Operation Northwest, ridership increased by 40 percent, while on Operation Northeast,[4] ridership almost quadrupled.

During the period between 1962 and 1970, the PSIC, and later the Southeastern Pennsylvania Transportation Authority (SEPTA), which assumed a regional transportation planning and operating role in 1965, continued to improve Philadelphia commuter service largely by putting modern, air-conditioned, comfortable commuter cars into service. These additions to rolling stock included 75 high performance, multiple-unit Silverliners and 12 new Budd Co. rail diesel cars. Eventually the new fleet will have a total of 144 new cars replacing more than 200 cars over 50 years old. Astounding to the railroads, this improvement program not only produced fare box results but also some significant advantages operationally. The Reading and the PRR experienced much lower maintenance costs which saved the line an average of $9,105 per car. For the contemplated fleet of 144 new cars, this would amount to an estimated annual savings of over $1.3 million in maintenance alone. They also incurred lower operating costs because of the smaller fleet size and larger capacities of the new cars.

The overwhelming fact about this Philadelphia story is that on all commuter systems where no improvements had taken place, ridership had been steadily lost up to 20 percent over mid-1950 levels; but on the six commuter lines that were upgraded and improved under the Philadelphia plan, ridership has improved an average of 62 percent since 1962. Significantly, 60 percent of these new riders were diverted from auto travel, while the balance was made up of new passengers and people attracted from other lines.

Almost riding on the coattails of the commuter "experiments" was the implementation of the new Lindenwold line which commenced service in January 1969 with 14.5 miles serving Camden and parts of southern New Jersey. There were many advantages in developing the new line, not the least of which was the fact that it reached out to a section of New Jersey that offered ample room for new suburban housing. Moreover, the basic objective of the new system's design was to furnish superior transportation, and several of the outstanding features of that design may explain its success. These include a grade-separated roadway; minimum noise levels; clean and airy elevated structures and stations with an attractive appearance; provision for protected parking under the elevated structures; an automatic fare collection system that requires less than a minute; and frequent daily, weekend, and night service. The trains are high performance with a rate of acceleration of 3 mph and top speed of 75 mph. Further, the train is run by an automatic train operation (ATO) system which controls the speeds to suit curves, grades, and other special conditions. The same system provides uniform dynamic braking, blends it with the air-brake system at lower speeds, and programs station stops within a tolerance of a few feet at the platform.

The Lindenwold line, although a commuter rail line by geography, was considered to be a hybrid system in which essentially commuter cars perform as high-speed rapid transit vehicles.

Benefits of Expansion and Improvement of Philadelphia's Commuter System

1. *User benefits*. Motorists driving from Lindenwold to Broad Street in the center of Philadelphia can make the trip through average traffic in 45 minutes. The bus trip takes 60 minutes. The actual running time of the Lindenwold line is 22.4 minutes. For almost 40,000 riders a day it offers a quiet, smooth, fast, safe, clean, and comfortable journey to and from work. Even those who still drive receive a significant benefit, because highway traffic congestion is reduced.

Economically, users of the Lindenwold line pay only 60 cents for the 14.5 miles. Gas, wear and tear on the car, parking fees of about $2.75 per day, and 50 cents worth of bridge tolls make the 60-cent train fare a bargain. It was estimated that commuters would save about $4 per day, or $1,000 per year, on commuting costs. Along with this is the benefit of ample free parking at the terminal and intermediate stations and a shorter travel time.

In terms of security, each station is watched by at least one television camera, monitored 24 hours a day from a central control station. Although attendants are not constantly present, security units are dispatched to any station in which vandalism or crime is observed. In addition, a special telephone line links the passengers with the monitoring room should they need help.

2. *Operator benefits*. The attitude toward marketing the Lindenwold line is somewhat unique in the commuter transportation industry. The Authority spent $160,000—3 percent of gross revenues—in 1970 on advertising and promotional campaigns with the idea that professionally handled advertising would speed the growth of patronage and enable the Lindenwold line to break even on operating expenses as soon as possible.[5] Currently, at 40,000 passengers per day, the line has surpassed this objective and hopefully will be able to even cover debt service in the revenue bonds in the near future. Planners feel that as soon as a sensible set of bus feeder routes are worked out, the line should absorb well up over 50,000 passengers per day—giving the DRPA a profit. Another first for the

DRPA is the use of bridge tolls across the crowded Delaware River crossings to subsidize the existence of the Lindenwold line, thus using highway revenues to help reduce highway congestion.

Minimization of operating costs was a major concern in designing the system, and close attention was given to automation. Automatic Train Operation (ATO) requires that only one employee, the train attendant, be on each train. ATO also has enabled the system to cut three minutes off of each round trip, thus reducing the need for equipment and increasing utilization. It has also better enabled the line to absorb the unusually short peak-period loads, which reach a maximum of more than 7,000 passengers between 5:00 and 5:30 P.M. Another operating improvement was the simple installation of cross-over tracks just west of the Lindenwold stations, chopping another four minutes off the round trip time. In addition, the complete automation of ticketing functions allows stations to go virtually unattended, also reducing personnel costs. Further, the central control tower regulates all car movements and power distribution, requiring only three men.

The cars and shops are designed for rapid simplified maintenance, repair, and testing. Computerized data systems also facilitate the diagnosis of maintenance problems, and an integrated EDP system provides a battery of operating and top management control reports.[6] In sum, the new methods and techniques permit the line to carry approximately 10,000,000 passengers annually with a total organization of only 225 people, in comparison to a comparable commuter railroad carrying 13,500,000 passengers with 755 people.

3. *Community benefits.* The Lindenwold line carries more people into the CBD during the peak hours than the Schuylkill Expressway does; and in terms of capital cost to the area, with ultimate capacity equal to more than two four-lane expressways, the Lindenwold line would cost only one-quarter as much. In addition, the land necessary for its construction required less than 10 percent of that necessary for a highway of the same person movement capacity.[7]

Finally, a significant community benefit of the Lindenwold line is in the opening of new areas of development in Philadelphia and Camden suburbs. This is important because of the tremendous density of other suburbs to the north and west of Philadelphia and industrial developments to the south. Construction on the Lindenwold line had hardly begun before new housing developments, apartment buildings, and shopping centers began all over the line. For example, Rouse Company, developers of Columbia, Maryland, began construction for a 392 acre, $80 million "downtown in the country" development near Lindenwold. It will include hotels, offices, four big department stores, 150 shops, and some 2,000 apartments and town house residences by 1976.

Summary

The Philadelphia-Lindenwold line has supplied a range of significant user benefits, including notable time savings over automobile or busing alternatives.

Other benefits are a quiet, safe, clean, comfortable trip for users, with reduced auto congestion and time savings possible for the remaining automobile travelers. Substantial savings are possible over automobile travel cost. Operator benefits also have resulted from the greater-than-anticipated ridership which was attributed to a professional advertising campaign. The operating authority subsidizes the line with bridge toll revenues, which also assist in the reduction of highway auto congestion, and operating costs have been minimized through the application of automation technology both in equipment and station design and operation.

Community benefits include opening new suburban areas for development, thereby potentially relieving the pressure on existing high density suburbs north and west of the city and industrial concentrations to the south. Diverse real estate development is under way.

Not specifically treated above were equality of access, employment, and environmental impact from the new line, for which information was not available. The benefits to travelers from outside of the Philadelphia region were not considered to be relevant. Finally, airport access is an issue in Philadelphia, but one which is considered secondary to basic improvements in public transit.

**Part III
Findings and Conclusions
of This Study**

7

Findings and Conclusions

The Basic Questions for Decisionmakers

In the Introduction to this volume, a basic question was posed: Should urban transportation policy be directed toward making provision solely or very heavily for the highway/private auto mode or should increasing provisions be made for developing, expanding, and/or improving one or more of the public transit modes?

As work on the study progressed, it became evident that four subsidiary or related questions needed to be addressed in order to fully analyze the policy implications of the basic issue. The first question (actually the same as the original issue) is whether public transportation should be increasingly pursued as a good alternative to the highway/auto mode to solve the problems of urban transportation. The second and third questions are related to breaking down the analysis of public transit in terms of time considerations (that is, are conventional systems of public transportation good alternatives, or does the answer lie with the future development of advanced technological systems?) and in terms of mode considerations (that is, do fixed guideway systems offer a good alternative or should increasing provision be made for other than fixed guideway?). Finally, the basic issue is approached from the financial aspect in terms of the desirability of using federal Highway Trust Fund (HTF) revenues for application to public transit.

The next section will examine each of these questions and analyze them with respect to the findings of the study.

The Findings of the Study

Under this subheading we shall examine each of the questions raised above and analyze them with respect to the findings of this study.

1. *Should public transit be increasingly pursued as a good alternative to the highway/auto mode of urban transportation?*

The question of whether public transit is a good alternative to the highway/ auto mode hinges in large part on the broad urban goals listed in the Introduction to this volume. The first factor to consider is whether the goals of

121

more equitable income distribution, revitalization of the economic base, increased participation in urban opportunities, improved social welfare, and improved quality of urban environment are all-inclusive in terms of the perspective of the policymaker. In addition, some weights should, in reality, be applied to these goals in order to arrive at a definitive answer to this first question.

This latter statement is linked closely to the use of goal achievement analysis as explained in the Introduction. The process of ranking goals results in a concomitant shift in the relative importance of the transportation objectives as the means of reaching a specific goal. Since public transit has less impact on certain objectives, its value as an alternative depends ultimately on the outcome of the weighting process. As also mentioned in the Introduction, it is not the purpose of this study to either rank the broad urban goals or to give a final and absolute "yes" or "no" on the issue of public transit as the better alternative. We will, however, review our findings from Parts I and II with respect to clearly discernible benefits (that is, realizations of objectives) that can be developed from the use of public transit systems.

Transportation Objectives Relating to
Impact from Public Transit

Increased equality of access to urban opportunities for the poor, the elderly, the young, and the handicapped. The importance of public transit to persons who are poor, aged, young, and/or handicapped and thereby unable to obtain a driver's license or own a car is supported by the high percentage of captive ridership experienced on most existing transit systems. People falling within one or more of these categories comprise 25 percent of our total population of more than 52 million people, and they are largely concentrated in the center cities. In every system for which we were able to obtain specific information on the makeup of ridership, these captive riders accounted for between 30 and 80 percent of the transit users. The evidence indicates that these persons gain in economic and psychological welfare from public transit systems which provide access to employment centers, discount retail stores, health and educational facilities, and cultural and social events. Where adequate transit service is not available to captive riders, investigations—such as those conducted by Project FIND—have found that needs and demands are very important, ranking second only to the problem of having sufficient income to obtain food, clothing, and shelter essentials.

Time savings. For a large portion of our middle- and upper-income people, time is a valuable commodity. In two well-documented cases, savings in commuting time was the most important factor influencing the diversion of choice riders from automobile to transit commuting. Public transit systems which run on either exclusive bus lanes or fixed guideways can realize time-savings over the highway/auto mode, as has been exemplified by the cases of the Shirley Highway lane, the I-95/Lincoln Tunnel approach lane, the Lindenwold line, the Skokie Swift, parts of Philadelphia's SEPTA system, and so forth. Rapid rail systems have a double time-savings advantage both in operating on exclusive rights-of-way and in being unaffected by adverse weather conditions.

Savings on vehicle ownership and operating costs. Travel by public transit can provide the user with a direct savings on vehicle operating costs. In some cases it can also eliminate the necessity to buy a car or invest in a second car. For families which can only afford one car, it means that transportation is available to the wife during the week for shopping trips and social activities. Commuting by means of transit systems can also eliminate parking fees, which, especially in the larger center cities, can be a significant added expense.

Increased safety. Each year automobile accidents claim approximately 55,000 lives and are the cause of serious injuries to about two million more persons. In contrast, rapid transit has an average of one accident per 30-million riders and an overall safety record which is 75 times better than the automobile, on a passenger-mile-traveled basis. Not only does transit directly benefit the objective of increased safety; it also has indirect advantages. By diverting commuters from automobiles, general highway traffic flow is improved, thus increasing safety for motorists and their passengers.

Operator benefits resulting from improved systems. Better equipment and improved management systems can create savings for transit operators both in terms of maintenance costs and operating costs. Improved crime prevention devices and techniques can also reduce monetary losses and incidents of personal injury, while increasing confidence in the system as a safe mode of urban transportation. Advances in equipment design and automated systems can provide direct impact on the financial status of public transportation, in addition to providing a safer and smoother running working environment for transit employees. Benefits to operator, in turn, have a favorable indirect impact, by increasing time savings, improving riding comfort, and insuring the vitality of the system to provide a needed service.

Increased benefits to nontransit travelers. Experience has shown that transit has two principal types of impact on nontransit travelers. For motorists, transit—through the diversion process—can help to reduce automobile and parking congestion, in addition to impacting favorably on the environment, shared by both the motorist and the transit rider, through lessening of air pollution and reduction in noise levels. Another impact of transit on noncommuting travelers is to provide better airport access, as illustrated in Cleveland. In this city, persons going to the airport have the choice of a relatively inexpensive and swift means of reaching their destination by rapid rail, while motorists face less highway congestion when driving to the airport.

Increased employment. As is the case with several other objectives, public transit can have both direct and indirect impacts on a specific area's employment picture. The highway industry itself generates employment opportunities in construction, administration, operations, maintenance, and repairs. Thus, indirectly public transit can provide a vital link between people and jobs, a factor which has particular significance with respect to lower income workers (for example, the cited case of the increase in the Sacramento welfare roles projected from a rise in unemployment as the result of a threatened discontinuation of bus service) and to isolated ghetto areas (for example, the McCone Commission findings on Watts).

Improved land-use planning and real estate development. The real estate development booms which have grown up along the routes of the Toronto and San Francisco rapid rail systems provide evidence of the impact which a fixed guideway system can have on improved land values and increased real estate investment. In both urban areas, a physical and economic revitalization have been directly attributable to a new rail transit network. Improved land-use planning takes two forms. One is the rather traditional view that fixed guideways transit is an important planners' tool for reinforcing existing patterns and trends in land development. This is particularly true with respect to growth along corridors, as in the case of San Francisco and the BART system. A newer approach to land-use planning which centers on rail transit involves the concept of multiuse and air rights. The Department of City Planning for the City of New York is currently investigating potential air rights development over several rights-of-way within the five boroughs.

Less air pollution. Statistics cited in Part I of this volume show that now and throughout the decade, air pollution will remain one of the major problems facing our urban areas. The largest percentage of all but two of the most deleterious emitted pollutants are released by automobiles. The impact which rapid transit can have on reducing air pollution has not been scientifically documented for specified systems; nevertheless, in terms of reducing the number of automobiles on the road, there are important implications for the benefits of public transit as a means of improving the quality of the air and, consequently, the health of urban residents.

Reduced noise levels. While general automobile traffic is not responsible for excessive noise levels in terms of A-scale decibel measurements, the congested nature of driving conditions in urban areas, increased horn-honking due to stop-and-go driving, and the effect which large center-city buildings have in echoing and channeling noise gives added dimensions to the automobile as a noise generator in city environments. In contrast, new technology in urban transit is producing equipment which is virtually noiseless. Tests on BART equipment and new buses being demonstrated in California are examples of these.

Transportation Objectives—Limitations
Considered in Making the Modal Choice

With respect to impact on the transportation objectives discussed in the preceding pages, it is clear that public transit in terms of objectives achieved is a superior alternative to the highway/auto mode. Also, it is equally clear that the various types of public transit do not rank equally among one another in meeting urban transportation objectives. In the paragraphs which follow, we shall review the objectives, however, from the perspective of limitations and qualifications to be considered in evaluating and weighting the modal choice.

Equality of access and increased safety from accidents. Compared to the alternative of highway/auto mode, public transit ranks highest with respect to its impact on the objectives of equality of access and safety from accidents. In the case of the former, the very term captive rider implies a person who has no real choice with respect to highway/auto versus public transit modes. The more than 52 million people who make up the captive ridership are the poor, ghetto residents, the elderly, and the handicapped—those segments of our population most in need of greater equity with respect to job, educational, and social opportunities. Yet, to date, no means of adopting the private automobile mode to service the poor, elderly, and handicapped has been conceptualized or demonstrated. Regarding the transportation of captive riders to employment centers, rapid rail and bus transit rank about equally; rapid rail offers greater capacity in dense, congested urban areas, while bus transit assumes importance in regions where population is more dispersed or employment centers are widely scattered. With respect to safety from accidents, the greater advantages of transit over automobile travel are a matter of public record. The number of deaths per million passenger miles is 5.3 for autos, .19 for buses, and .07 for trains. Improved technology in automated train control and the use of two-way communications devices in buses are currently being introduced in some areas. Such developments will augment the benefits of public transit as the safest means of urban transportation.

Time savings. Time savings from the use of public transit can vary widely depending on both the specific system and mode. For example, passengers may save 20 minutes in travel time each way by commuting into New York on the I-95 exclusive bus lane, but would realize no time savings in the case of buses which do not operate on exclusive lanes and which face the same traffic delays as automobiles. Another illustration is a swift and efficient rapid rail system that offers substantial time savings when compared to auto travel between the same two points. The rider, however, may end up spending more time when traveling by transit if the station is not convenient to his ultimate destination, or if headways are sufficiently long to cause loss of time in waiting for initial pickups and in transferring.

Savings on vehicle ownership and operating costs. Since in many instances persons using public transit also own cars, savings on vehicle ownership costs become a real consideration only with respect to the poor or those who without transit would buy a second car. In most cases, operating cost savings will accrue to transit riders; the notable exception to this is the case of commuter rail systems where the price of a monthly pass may come close to eliminating any increased savings resulting from not operating a car.

Benefits to operators. Objectives under this category are not discussed here, since the highway/auto mode does not present any alternative for this kind of impact.

Benefits to nontransit travelers. This objective is also not discussed here in terms of improved traffic flow, because this impact assumes a balanced transportation system characterized by the availability of both the automobile and transit modes. Airport access, however, is a different issue. From the evidence at hand, the impact of public transit on persons going to airports varies proportionally to the amount of highway congestion along the airport access route. In the case of Cleveland, the rapid rail extension was able to reduce auto congestion, thereby offering time and cost savings to both motorists and transit riders. In the case of Tokyo, on the other hand, the time savings and convenience of the rapid transit access line have not been great enough to divert many people from the highway/auto mode.

Increased employment. Employment impact from public transit, as contrasted with the highway/auto mode, is most strongly evidenced in providing access to jobs for persons who are too poor to own a car or who are too old, young, or physically handicapped to drive a car. A careful analysis of the entire employment-impact issue is somewhat hindered by the lack of careful surveying or documentation—at least for any large-scale system—of actual employment-related benefits generated by bus, rapid rail, or commuter systems. Thus, this is a highly unresolved issue. One might, for example, ask why the ghettos of Harlem and Bedford Stuyvesant still exist, if, as claimed, public transit can break through the isolation of the ghettos. A partial answer might be that reverse haul from those New York slums to the large semiskilled and unskilled industrial employment centers in New Jersey and Westchester County has been characterized by limited service and high prices for commuting tickets. The PATH system may be having some impact, but to date there is insufficient information for a full assessment.

Improved environmental quality. Under this heading are three objectives—better land use and increased real estate development; reduced air pollution; and less noise. In the first instance, the case for fixed guideway systems is very favorable. For example, in Boston the South Shore extension was developed along an old right-of-way, creating better transportation without disrupting existing land-use patterns. Air-right development also is an advantage associated with rail systems. There is a possibility, however, that fixed guideways can become a liability in areas experiencing rapid changes in both economic structure and the location of employment centers. With respect to air and noise pollution, new transit equipment is far superior to automobiles. Still, many systems, due to financial constraints, must rely on older equipment which does not rank very well in terms of reducing pollution levels.

2. *Are the advantages of conventional systems sufficient to justify large investments, or should increased investment be held off pending the further development of new systems?*

The findings of our study show that there are substantial benefits to be derived from conventional transit systems which, in terms of economic and social impact, support the case for immediate large capital investment in rapid rail or other transit modes. The social and economic impacts have been described at length in the preceding sections.

On the issue of conventional versus new-concept systems, the conventional systems have several advantages:

a. In most cases, land has already been acquired, and as in Boston and Cleveland, existing rights-of-ways can be improved or reused.
b. An advantage related to the first is that conventional systems conform to and reinforce existing patterns of development (for example, fixed guideway systems along concentrated development corridors, versus bus transit in areas where development has been dispersed).
c. The equipment used in conventional systems has generally been debugged from the technological standpoint.
d. New technology can be adapted to and used by conventional systems. Examples of this new technology include automatic train control, automatic fare collection equipment, methods of crime prevention, and, in the case of buses, antipollution devices.

In contrast, new systems such as personal rapid transit (PRT) and tracked air cushion vehicles (TACV) require equipment testing and demonstration, as well as further development of control and management systems.

3. *Are fixed guideway systems—in particular rapid rail—a worthwhile alternative in terms of being a risky long-term investment which may realize only a marginal benefit?*

Two arguments are sometimes raised with respect to fixed guideway systems being a poor capital investment alternative. The first argument is that present rail systems are obsolete, as evidenced by declining ridership figures. The second argument is that new systems fail to realize projected benefits and become quickly outdated.

In response to the first argument, the popular conception that rapid transit ridership has been declining in major cities simply is not true. There was a postwar decline in transit ridership for all modes and particularly for rapid transit, but this leveled off around 1963. For example, the Chicago rapid transit carried 111 million passengers in 1963 and 111 million in 1968, despite a 24 percent increase in the average fare. The Philadelphia rapid transit system carried 62 million passengers in 1963 and 70 million in 1968, with a 20 percent fare increase. In New York City, the rapid transit system carried 1,356 million passengers in 1963 and 1,306 million in 1968 despite a 33 percent increase in the average fare. Overall, subway and elevated systems carried 1.7 billion passengers in 1960 and 1.6 billion passengers in 1970; only a slight decline considering the increases in fares, general declines in service, and the large amount of new highway construction.

Moreover, rapid transit extension and improvement programs are predominantly characterized by ridership far in excess of original projections. For example, the Dan Ryan extension in Chicago, Cleveland's airport extension, and Boston's South Shore extension are presently carrying about twice as many passengers as were originally estimated.

In response to the argument against investment in new systems, the Toronto subway is existing proof that project benefits of significant magnitude (for example, land development, revitalization of the urban economy, and reduced street congestion) can be generated. It also provides support for the assertion that new systems do not quickly become obsolete. In terms of the land development and economic revitalization already visible, the BART system is providing support for the fact that similar benefits can be realized elsewhere in the United States.

4. *Is it desirable to use some HTF revenues for public transportation?*

This question must be answered in terms of two other questions: (i) Is it fair and socially equitable? (Who pays and who benefits from investments in urban public transportation?); and (ii) Is it good management?

It is often implied that Highway Trust Fund revenues should be sacrosanct vis-à-vis highway programs because it is not the public at large that is paying, but rather it is a special group that pays (and benefits)—the highway user. This line of argument is unfortunate. In fact, the general public and not some special group does provide most of the revenues.

Approximately three-quarters of the funds going into the HTF came from private auto taxes, and, as noted elsewhere in this volume, better than three-quarters of our populace owns or uses a car. In short this is not a specialized tax, rather it is a broad public levy. In fact, the only segment of our population that effectively does not pay into the HTF is that 20 to 25 percent of the population—poor, elderly, young, handicapped—that society is trying to explicitly help. Further, the high concentration of population (auto ownership and usage) in the metropolitan areas provides strong connection between metropolitan automobile "payers" and location of public transit.

Given that the public at large pays, does the public at large benefit? In fact, most segments of society benefit. As we documented in great detail in Parts I and II of this volume, and as summarized in an earlier section of this part, the benefits of the public transit alternative are pervasive and far-reaching. Because urban life itself is vastly improved, everybody in our urban areas benefits. Also, because the rider is now better served by his (public) transportation system he benefits. And the continuing auto driver saves times and faces less congestion. The city itself benefits economically from the increased revenue and employment derived from the public transit system, and socially from the improved access and physical appearance of our urban areas.

The nonpaying group mentioned above also clearly benefits and we as a society have made it clear we should and will help. Much public policy has already been directed toward assisting the disadvantaged in our society—poor, elderly, and handicapped—with tax revenues from the nation as a whole. Graduated income taxes, welfare programs, programs for the aging, vocational rehabilitation efforts, the poverty program, Headstart, manpower training, and so forth, are but a small example of the manifestations of public policy in redistributing income or tending toward equity in our society. The use of some HTF revenues for public transportation would simply be an additional technique for accomplishing an economically and socially equitable objective.

Is it good management to use HTF revenues for public transportation? All of the preceding analysis and description confirms the necessity for flexibility in attempting to solve our urban transportation problems. In some cases, rail rapid systems may not be the answer; in others, new highway construction and further dependence on the auto may make neither economic nor social sense. In any case, the decisionmaker must have both complete information from which to choose and the flexibility to use available funds to support and sustain that choice. This decision must be made on a specific situation-by-situation basis. If resources are separated and segregated (by public transit and highway), the ability to make a clearly desirable specific situation tradeoff simply is not possible. The use of HTF revenues for public transportation is good management.

The Conclusions of the Study

Our findings from Parts I and II of this study, when analyzed in terms of the questions raised in the first section of this part, permit the following conclusions to be drawn:

1. *Frequently, although not always, public transit is a good alternative to highways in urban areas.* It is not to be disputed that, on an individual basis, people clearly like the flexibility and convenience of cars. Nonetheless, it is also clear that there are broad social benefits to be gained by increased investment in public transit. These benefits include increased access for the poor, the elderly, the young, and the handicapped to urban opportunities; increased economic vitality through (i) better delivery of goods and services over less congested streets and (ii) better links between producers and consumers; and improvements in the quality of the urban environment due to more efficient land use and reduced levels of air and noise pollution.

2. *Within the category of public transit, conventional systems can provide a valuable contribution to solving urban transportation problems.* The demand for improved mobility in metropolitan regions is evidenced by the section on needs, included with each case study presented in Part II. Conventional systems can run over existing rights-of-way, and they have technologically reliable standards with respect to equipment and operations. This is not to say that investments should be solely for conventional systems to the detriment of advances in new-concept technology. What is stressed is that conventional systems can provide an answer to urgent existing problems which are increasing at such a rapid speed (for example, the rate of population growth on increasing congestion, less available land, and greater demand on transportation facilities) that to wait for new-concept technology to be fully developed may aggravate the situation beyond all hope of solution.

3. *Rapid rail transit as an alternative to the auto and bus modes, when examined in terms of the list of transportation objectives, ranks first in terms of total benefits in urban areas which are characterized by a relatively large and concentrated population.*

4. *The issue of using a portion of Highway Trust Fund revenues to support public transit has been approached in an indirect way by this study. Our findings indicate that this indeed would be a sensible policy decision.* The reasons for this are as follows:

   a. It would be an equitable use of highway tax revenues in that the persons who pay the taxes would also benefit from public transit through less congestion and improved quality of the environment.
   b. It would be a socially responsible allocation in that those who do not pay these taxes are primarily the underprivileged people in our society whom our government is dedicated to helping.

c. It would be an efficient use of funds in terms of principles of good management, enabling local governments to exercise greater flexibility by providing an increase in the options available to meet specific needs.

Observations

We have concluded that public transit is, in many cases, a desirable social and economic investment for meeting our urban transportation needs and reaching the broad urban goals discussed in the Introduction to this volume. This study was conceived of as the first phase of a broader, more systematic effect to delineate and support in greater detail the findings and conclusions previously described, as well as to examine the areas discussed later in this section. The guidelines for the decisionmaker presented in this section are not to be viewed as "cast in concrete" statements, but rather experiences and facts to keep in mind when considering the public transit alternative. There are several general observations which must be kept in mind in deciding what solution may be applicable to each particular urban transportation situation.

1. Public transit systems serve to realize some, but not all, of the objectives set forth previously in the report; clearly focusing on which of the objectives are to be reached is the important function of the decisionmaker.
2. No matter how technologically, economically, or socially desirable a system appears, the anticipated benefits will not occur if there are not enough riders. Ridership tests should be a vital part of any transit system decision.
3. The public transit alternative vis-à-vis the auto/highway choice should be evaluated in a framework of total impact, not just narrow economic formulae.

With the above general observations as background, the following guidelines were developed to help the decisionmaker identify with some specific situations and generalizations arising from this first-phase effort.

Fixed Guideway (Mostly Rail Rapid Transit)

1. Time savings should be measured and can be quite significant in areas where rail rapid transit bypasses congested bridges and highways.
2. In areas with large student commuter populations, a public transit system can introduce substantial saving in auto costs in addition to opening up educational opportunities for poor people.
3. Public transit opens up access for minorities to suburban and CBD employment centers (reverse commuting).
4. In situations where air pollution levels are high, both increased ridership and

diversion of existing auto/highway users are desirable results obtained from rail rapid transit.

5. Improvements in safety, comfort, and aesthetics both increase subway ridership and lower total social costs.
6. A rail rapid system needs more than a single CBD distribution point to reach its ridership potential.
7. Airport travel peaking hours may not be in the 8:00 to 10:00 A.M. or 4:00 to 6:00 P.M. peak rush hours, thus making possible better system utilization.
8. In areas where CBD land is at a premium, a public transit system will make larger buildings possible, increase the tax base, and make available land which would otherwise have been used for parking.
9. New service with unattractive and uncomfortable equipment will not divert riders or increase ridership.
10. High advertising expenditures stimulate rail rapid commuter transit and should be planned for.
11. A rapid rail commuter train has reverse flow of inner-city residents to jobs in the suburbs, which extends access to jobs by minority groups.
12. Rapid rail commuter saves on land requirements compared to highway/auto.
13. Extensive examination of demographic analysis to determine the extent of the captive populations, its transportation needs (quantity and time periods), and price elasticity should be conducted before any public transit decision is made.
14. A FAST, RELIABLE, AND CONVENIENT RAIL RAPID COMMUTER SERVICE WILL EXCEED EXPECTATIONS.

Highway Mode (Bus)

1. Minibus service provides important social and recreational access for teenagers, particularly on Saturday.
2. Smaller buses are better in terms of traffic flow than larger buses in congested central areas.
3. The appeal of high-speed exclusive bus lanes is derived from time savings and avoidance of the high costs of parking.
4. Buses can be equipped with antipollution devices to eliminate polluting fumes.
5. Dial-A-Ride concepts require extremely careful planning and progressive management and focus especially on the handicapped and the elderly.
6. Small buses reduce pollution in the CBD as compared with autos and larger buses.
7. Most express bus riders are diverted from auto commuting.
8. Free parking is necessary for attaining high levels of express bus ridership.
9. Express bus service can introduce significant time savings over regular bus service and can increase capacity available to the local service operator.

10. New bus purchases under the UMTA capital grant program reduce maintenance costs and increase ridership, primarily serving the elderly, poor, and handicapped.
11. Fare reductions and special fare arrangements, accompanied by improvements such as better service frequency, route extensions, and new equipment, can increase ridership and revenues.
12. Extensive examination of demographic analysis to determine the extent of the captive populations, their transportation needs (quantity and time periods), and price elasticity should be conducted before any public transit decision is made.

Future Steps

In completing Phase I of our study effort, we identified several areas where further examination would have a positive impact on the broader effort of assisting the decisionmaker and policymaker in the urban transportation field. The following list illustrates some areas for possible future exploration:

1. A system of relating and weighting many urban transportation issues—such as long-term development of new modes—according to the established objectives—such as equality of access for the poor—and finally to specific programs. The final output will be a quantitative measure of the desirability of alternative expenditure packages.
2. Present and alternative revenue distribution formulae/methods.
3. Federal, state, and local administrative structures designed to effectively manage joint highway and public transit funding.
4. Timing, roles, and authorities of levels of government in selecting among principal alternatives.
5. Ways and means of tying in to the various planning activities including the comprehensive planning requirements and the 1972 and 1974 studies of transportation needs.

All of the above have some major organizational and policy implications which must be clearly identified and resolved.

Notes

Notes

Introduction

1. Excellent discussions which compare the techniques of cost-benefit analysis and goal achievement analysis can be found in the following sources: Kenneth J. Arrow, "Criteria for Social Investment," *Water Resources Research*, First Quarter, 1965, pp. 1-9; James Vedder, "Planning Problems with Multidimensional Consequences," *Journal of the American Institute of Planners*, March 1970, pp. 112-19; Morris Hill, "A Method for the Evaluation of Transportation Plans," *Highway Research Record*, No. 180, 1967, pp. 21-34; Roland N. McKean, *Efficiency in Government Through Systems Analysis* New York: John Wiley, 1958; George Perazich and Leonard L. Fischman, "Methodology for Evaluating Costs and Benefits of Alternative Urban Transportation Systems," *Highway Research Record*, No. 48, 1966, pp. 59-93; A.R. Prest and R. Ruvey, "Cost Benefit Analysis–A Survey," *The Economic Journal*, December 1965.

2. The goals and objectives were drawn from or suggested by the following sources: Donald H. Elliott, Commissioner, Department of City Planning. The City of New York. (March, 1972, verbal statement.); Morris Hill, op. cit., pp. 26-27; George M. Smerk, "An Evaluation of Ten Years of Federal Policy in Urban Mass Transportation," *Transportation Journal*, pp. 49-50; Wilbur Smith and Associates, *Urban Transportation Concepts* (Cambridge: Arthur D. Little, Inc., Center City Transportation Project, September 1970), p. 45; George Perazich and Leonard L. Fischman, op. cit., p. 68.

Part I
Evaluation of the Impacts of Public Transit
on the Objectives of Urban Transportation

1. Joseph S. De Salvo, *Proceedings of a Conference on Regional Transportation Planning*, January 25-27, 1971. (Santa Monica, California: The Rand Corp., May 1971), p. 5. The terms "efficiency" and "equity" are defined as follows: An allocation of resources is "efficient" if there is no other allocation which would make at least one person better off without making anyone else worse off, and where "better off" is in terms of each individual's own preferences, not as they are perceived by someone else. An allocation of resources could be efficient, but the distribution might be undesirable from society's viewpoint. "Equity" exists when the allocation of resources is efficient and the associated distribution of income is acceptable to society.

2. Arthur D. Little, Inc., *Center City Transportation Studies*, Cambridge, 1970, Vol. I, p. 44.

3. Edmund H. Mantell, "Economic Biases in Urban Transportation Planning and Implementation," *Traffic Quarterly*, January 1971, pp. 117-28.

Chapter 1
User Benefits

1. Richard M. Nixon, "Special Revenue Sharing for Transportation" (The President's Message to Congress, March 18, 1971), *Federal Register*, March 22, 1971, pp. 498-502.

2. "Captive riders" are defined as those who for economic reasons have no car or those who have no car available for reasons other than economic (i.e., the non-drivers, including the young, the aged, the handicapped, and drivers whose cars are temporarily out of service). Contrasted to these are the "choice riders" who have cars available but prefer to use transit because of traffic congestion, parking costs, and other points of personal preference. (Alan M. Voorhees & Associates, Inc., *A Transit Improvement Program for the Utah Transit Authority*, McLean, Virginia, March 1971, p. 53.)

3. Parsons, Brinckerhoff, Tudor, Bechtel, Sverdrup & Parcel, *St. Louis Metropolitan Area: Rapid Transit Feasibility Study, Long-Range Program*, PB204-060, St. Louis, August 1971, pp. 79-80.

4. U.S. Congress, House Subcommittee of the Committee on Appropriations, *Hearings on Department of Transportation and Related Agencies Appropriations for 1972*, 91st Congress, 1st Session, Part I, p. 54.

5. Martin Wohl, "Current Mass-Transit Proposals: Answer to Our Commuter Problem?" *Civil Engineering—ASCE*, December 1971, p. 70.

6. U.S. Congress, op. cit.

7. Martin Wohl, op. cit., p. 70.

8. Massachusetts Institute of Technology Urban Systems Laboratory, USL-TR-71-03, *Dial-a-Ride: An Overview of a New Demand-Responsive Transportation System*, Cambridge, Mass., March 1971, p. 11.

9. Milton S. Baum, Albert Gutowsky, and Gerald Rucker, *Cost and Benefit Evaluation of the Sacramento Transit Authority*, Interim Technical Report #4, Sacramento State College, October 1970, p. 27.

10. Automobile Manufacturers Association, *1967 Automobile Facts and Figures*, Detroit, 1967, p. 36.

11. U.S. Congress, House Subcommittee of the Committee on Appropriations, *Hearings of Department of Transportation and Related Agencies Appropriations for 1972*, 91st Congress, 1st Session, 1971, Part III, p. 222.

12. Herr and Fleisher, "The Mobility of the Poor," paper presented at the Transportation and Poverty Conference, American Academy of Arts and Science (June 7, 1968), based on data by the Eastern Massachusetts Regional Planning Project, Massachusetts Department of Public Works.

13. Boston Urban Foundation Study, *Center City*, 1969.

14. Floyd, "Using Transportation to Alleviate Poverty: A Progress Report on Experiments Under Urban Mass Transportation Act," Transportation and Poverty Conference, June 7, 1968.

15. Herr and Fleisher, op. cit., p. 7.

16. U.S. Congress, House Subcommittee on Housing of the Committee on Banking and Currency, *Hearings on HR 6663, S.3154, HR 7006, HR 13463, HR 16261*, March 1970, p. 93.

17. *People, Jobs, and Transportation*, December 1969, p. 94.

18. Pittsburgh Regional Planning Association, *Westmoreland County Comprehensive Plan Study*, (Preliminary Report), Volume II, p. 47.

19. Alan M. Voorhees, "The Changing Role of Transportation in Urban Development," *Traffic Quarterly* 23, October 1969: 530.

20. Whitney Young, Jr., "Transportation: Making Cities Work for People," *Official Proceedings of the Fourth International Conference on Urban Transportation* (Pittsburgh: Urban Transit Council, 1971), p. 121.

21. U.S. Congress, *Hearings on HR 6663, S.3150, HR 7006, HR 13463, HR 16261*, p. 121.

22. Louis J. Pignatoro and Edmund J. Cantilli, "Transportation and the Aging," *Traffic Engineering*, July 1971, p. 42.

23. U.S. Congress, *Hearings on HR 6663, S.3154, HR 7006, HR 13463, HR 16261*, op. cit., p. 563.

24. Ibid., pp. 430, 431.

25. Ashford and Holloway, op. cit., pp. 47 and 49.

26. Carnegie-Mellon University, Transportation Research Institute, *Latent Demand for Urban Transportation*, Pittsburgh, May 1968, p. 15.

27. U.S. Department of Transportation, Urban Mass Transit Administration, *Capital Grant Approval Memo for Project CAL-UTG-39* (April 9, 1971).

28. U.S. Congress, *Hearings on HR 6663, S.3154, HR 7006, HR 13463, HR 16261*, op. cit., p. 564.

29. Ibid., p. 565.

30. Ibid., p. 429.

31. Carnegie-Mellon University, op. cit., p. 24.

32. U.S. Congress, *Hearings on HR 6663, S.3154, HR 7006, HR 13463, HR 16261*, op. cit., p. 567.

33. Ibid., p. 432.

34. Baltimore Department of Transit and Transportation, *Job Express Transportation*, June 1971, pp. 27-30.

35. Columbus, Georgia, *Columbus Youth Opportunity 1970 Information Package*.

36. Ashford, op. cit., p. 39.

37. Town of Hempstead, *The Merrick Minibus: A Small Feeder Bus Operation for Commuters*, Final Report, Mass Transportation Demonstration Project, NY-MTD-11, May 1971.

38. Abt Associates. *Travel Barriers: Transportation Needs of the Handicapped*, Cambridge, August 1969, p. 2.

39. Carnegie-Mellon University, op. cit., p. 57.

40. Ibid.

41. Abt Associates, op. cit., p. 2.

42. Ibid.

43. Alan M. Voorhees, op. cit., p. 528.

44. U.S. Congress, *Hearings on Department of Transportation and Related Agencies Appropriations for 1972*, op. cit., Part III, p. 273.

45. Only 7.9 percent of the respondents did not think rapid transit was a good idea, generally because of the expense involved, and 15 percent of the respondents had not made up their minds on the subject. (Atlanta Metropolitan Rapid Transit Authority, *The Atlanta Plan: Rapid Transit for the People*, July 1970, Appendix IV, p. 3.)

46. Resource Management Corporation, *Theory and Implementation of Cost and Benefit Analysis of Transportation Systems: The Northeast Corridor Transportation Project*, Maryland, 1969, p. 6.18.

47. Baum, op. cit., p. 3.

48. Stanford Research Institute, *Benefit/Cost Analysis of the Five-Corridor Rapid Transit System for Los Angeles*, California, 1968, p. 14.

49. Development Research Associates, *Benefits to the Federal Government from the Adapted Regional Metro System* (Technical Appendix), prepared for Washington Metropolitan Area Transit Authority, Washington, D.C., October 1968, p. 26.

50. Stanford Research Institute, op. cit., p. 20.

51. Parsons, Brinckerhoff et al., op. cit., p. 81.

52. Ibid.

53. Stanford Research Institute, op. cit., p. 16.

54. Stone and Youngberg, *Rapid Transit for the Bay Area*, October 1961, p. 30.

55. Newsletter published by Liberty Mutual Insurance Company for the first quarter of 1972.

56. U.S. Congress, *Hearings on Department of Transportation Appropriations for 1972*, op. cit., Part I, p. 12.

57. Parsons, Brinckerhoff et al., op. cit., p. 90.

58. Resource Management Corp., op. cit., p. 6.19.

59. Ibid.

60. Ibid.

61. Wilbur Smith & Associates, *The Potential for Bus Rapid Transit* (Detroit: Automobile Manufacturing Association, 1970), p. 5.

Chapter 2
Operator Benefits

1. "National Survey on Exact Fare System Shows Sharp Crime Drop," *Police*, December 1971, p. 12.

2. A letter from the Cleveland Transit System to William Hurd, Assistant Administrator of the Urban Mass Transportation Administration, dated June 11, 1971.

3. "National Survey on Exact Fare System," op. cit.

4. Stanford Research Institute and the University of California, *Reductions of Robberies and Assaults of Bus Drivers*, December 1970, Vol. I, p. 11.

5. Ibid., p. 17.

Chapter 3
Community Benefits

1. Stanford Research Institute, op. cit., p. 37.

2. U.S. Congress, *Hearings on HR 6663*, op. cit., p. 106.

3. Charles D. Baker, *High-Speed Ground Transportation Journal*, May 1970, p. 314.

4. U.S. Congress, *Hearings on HR 17755*, op. cit., p. 877.

5. U.S. Congress Senate Subcommittee on Housing and Urban Affairs of the Committee on Banking and Currency, 91st Congress, 1st Session, *Hearings on S.676, S.1032, S.2656, S.2821, S.3154*, 1969, p. 19.

6. Statement by the Secretary of Transportation, Housing Subcommittee Hearings on HR 6663, p. 121.

7. Cuyahoga County, Regional Planning Commission, *Cleveland Hopkins Airport Access Study*, survey results, prepared for U.S. Department of Transportation, June 1970, p. v.

8. Ibid.

9. "Tiny Bus Spurs City Shopping," *Business Week*, September 12, 1964, pp. 196-97.

10. Stanford Research Institute, op. cit., 120b, p. 29.

11. For further discussion of transit's impact on the poor and ghetto residents, see Chapter 1, the section on "Equality of Access."

12. Memo: Amend. No. 2 to Project No. CAL-UTG-19, November 24, 1971.

13. Stanford Research Institute, op. cit., p. 20c.

14. "Aerospace Crowds Into Mass Transit," *Business Week*, September 18, 1971, pp. 20-21.

15. American Transit Association, *Transit Fact Book '70-'71*, p. 10, Table #11.

16. Parsons, Brinckerhoff et al., op. cit.

17. G. Warren Heenan, "The Economic Effect of Rapid Transit on Real Estate Development," *The Appraisal Journal*, April 1968.

18. Parsons, Brinckerhoff et al., op. cit., p. 75.

19. Heenan, op. cit., p. 216.

20. Terrell W. Hill, "The Impact of Transit: The Central Business District," *Transportation: Lifeline of an Urban Society*, Pittsburgh Urban Transit Council,

Fourth International Conference on Urban Transportation, Official Proceedings, 1969, pp. 140-46.

21. Ibid.

22. Parsons, Brinckerhoff et al., op. cit., p. 76.

23. Stanford, op. cit., p. 167.

24. Heenan, op. cit., pp. 215-16.

25. Stanford, op. cit., Appendix J.

26. Parsons, Brinckerhoff et al., op. cit., p. 78.

27. William Barr, *Parking: Public vs. Private*, in "A Look at Urban Transportation," by Ardie Ames, reprinted from *Nation's Cities*, July 1, 1965, p. 14.

28. Simpson and Curtin, *Public Transit Master Plan*, Philadelphia, 1969, p. 88.

29. Development Research Associates, op. cit., p. 11.

30. Parsons, Brinckerhoff et al., op. cit., p. 79.

31. Stanford, op. cit., p. 34.

32. Simpson, op. cit., p. 87.

33. Stanford, op. cit., p. 175.

34. Ibid., p. 36.

35. Wilbur, op. cit., pp. 6-16.

36. Edwin W. Hauser, Leonard B. West, Jr., A. Richard Schleicher, "Fundamental Air Pollution Considerations for Urban and Transportation Planners," *Traffic Quarterly*, January 1972, pp. 73-74.

37. In 1966, the U.S. Surgeon General stated: "There is no doubt that air pollution is a factor which contributes to illness, disability, and death from chronic respiratory diseases." (cited in Kamrass, Crane, Hughes, and Parker, *Concepts for Evaluating Center City Transportation Programs and Projects*, Virginia, December 1969, p. 38).

38. Stanford Research Institute, op. cit., p. 188.

39. E.N. Dodson, "Cost-Benefit Scales for Urban Transportation," *Systems Analysis of Urban Transportation*, Vol. 3, California: General Research Corp., January 1968, p. 121.

40. Resource Management Corp., op. cit. Also see David W. Rasmussen, *Joint Development: An Economic Input*, Tallahassee, Florida, Florida State University, June 1970, p. 20 ff.

41. Resource Management Corp., op. cit., pp. 6.24-6.25.

42. Stanford Research Institute, op. cit., p. 190.

43. This was considered to be the upper limit of the benefit, since any more devices on the market between now and 1980 would reduce the remaining pollutants to an even greater extent. Stanford Research Institute, op. cit., p. 190.

44. Sacramento Bee, July 27, 1968, p. D-18, reporting on research of Dr. Lowell L. Coulson, Professor of Meteorology, University of California at Davis, as cited in Milton S. Baum, op. cit., p. 2.

45. Charles D. Baker, op. cit., p. 137.

46. Noise is measured as root mean square (rms) pressure. The ratio (multiplied by 10) between a particular noise pressure and a standard low pressure (0.0002 dynes/cm^2) is called the sound pressure (SPL) and is commonly expressed in decibels (db). M. Kamrass, op. cit., p. 61.

47. Stanford Research Institute, op. cit., pp. 42-43.

Chapter 4
Rapid Rail Transit

1. "Bay Area Rapid Transit," *Modern Railroads*, January 1972, p. 59.

2. EBASCO Services, Inc., *San Francisco Bay Area Rapid Transit District: Rapid Transit System Economic Review*, June 1961.

3. Parsons, Brinckerhoff, Tudor, Bechtel, *San Francisco Bay Area Rapid Transit District*, Technical Report #12, Summary, Demonstration Project, January 1970.

4. "BART: The Prototype Route Pays Off," *Railway Age*, May 10, 1971, p. 25.

5. Institute for Rapid Transit, *The Economic Justification of Rapid Transit*, Proceedings of the Second Annual Meeting, Washington, D.C., May 10, 1963, pp. 7-8.

6. U.S. Congress, *Hearings on H.R. 6663*, op. cit., p. 202.

7. David G. Hammond, "BART Demonstration Programs," *Transportation Engineering Journal of ASCE*, November 1971, pp. 632-33.

8. Ibid., pp. 636-37.

9. Ibid., pp. 639-40.

10. U.S. Congress, *Hearings on H.R. 6663*, op. cit., p. 204.

11. Hammond, op. cit., pp. 642-43.

12. "BART, Catalyst for Bay Area Planning," *Rapid Transit*, 1968, pp. 3-5.

13. Joe Asher, "If Transit Comes, Can a Real Estate Developer Be Far Behind?", *Railway Age*, November 8, 1971, pp. 32-33.

14. Institute for Rapid Transit, op. cit., p. 9.

15. Statement of B.R. Stokes, General Manager, San Francisco BARTD, U.S. Congress, Senate Subcommittee on Housing and Urban Affairs of the Committee on Banking and Currency, 91st Congress, 1st Session, *Hearings on S.676, S.2656, S.2821, and S.3154*, 1969, p. 251.

16. Bay Area Rapid Transit District, "BART and the Ghettos," *Rapid Transit*, (Summer 1969), Volume II, No. 3.

17. U.S. Department of Transportation, *Broad and Columbia Subway Development Study*, 1971.

18. Philadelphia Model Cities Program, *Application for a Mass Transportation Capital Improvement Grant*, March 30, 1970, p. 8.

19. DeLeuw, Cather & Company, *Cleveland Transit System: Feasibility Study, Euclid Avenue Extension and the Downtown Distribution Loop*, 1959.

20. George F. Wiggers, U.S. Department of Transportation, "Cleveland Rail Transit Airport Service," *Highway Research Board*, #330, 1970, pp. 21-24.

21. Development Research Associates, op. cit.

22. "A New Transit for Washington, D.C.," *Railway Age*, January 4, 1965, p. 18.

23. Development Research Associates, op. cit.

24. Alan M. Voorhees & Associates, Inc., as cited in Development Research Associates, op. cit.

25. Chicago Transit Authority, *Chicago Central Area Transit Planning Study*, Vol. II, Chicago, 1970.

26. U.S. Congress, *Hearings on H.R. 6663, S.3154, H.R. 7006, H.R. 13463, H.R. 16261*, op. cit., p. 219.

27. Housing Subcommittee Report, *H.R. 663*, "Prepared Statement of Ralph Petratos, Chicago, Illinois."

28. "Boston Mounts a $340 Million Attack on Transportation Confusion," *Engineering News-Record*, September 1, 1966, pp. 32-34.

29. Ron Muehlberger, MBTA, "Public Transit Access to Airports," Highway Research Board, 1969. (Presently if one wishes to go from Cambridge to Logan Airport, a distance of six miles, from three to five transfers are necessary.)

30. "A Big Drop in Public Transit Use," *American City*, October 1965, p. 137.

31. "Public Transport in Five Great Metropolitan Areas—Part II," *American City*, July 1960, pp. 131-32.

32. "New Cars Cut Costs for Boston," *Railway Age*, March 4, 1963, p. 16.

33. DeLeuw, Cather & Company, *Report to the Old Colony Area Transportation Commission on Plans for Improved Suburban Transit*, April 1959, p. 23.

34. Joe Asher, op. cit.

Chapter 5
Bus Transit

1. *Passenger Transport*, January 7, 1972, p. 1.

2. Appropriation Subcommittee Hearings 1972, Part 3, p. 266.

3. Appropriation Committee Hearings, *H.R. 9667*, p. 681.

4. *Passenger Transport*, op. cit., p. 2.

5. Administrator Carlos C. Villarreal, Urban Mass Transportation Administration, "The UMTA Bus Program," *Department of Transportation News*.

6. *Passenger Transport*, op. cit.

7. Cited in Beach W. Aten et al., *WMA Transit Company*, Urban Transportation Center, Consortium of Universities, Washington, August 1970, p. 43.

8. Appropriation Committee Hearings, 1972, p. 9.

9. "Innovative Transit Planning Attracts Riders," *Passenger Transport*, January 21, 1972, p. 1.

10. The Port of New York Authority, *A Plan for an Exclusive Bus Lane on Interstate Route 495 from the New Jersey Turnpike to the Lincoln Tunnel*, January 1967, p. 2.

11. *Passenger Transport*, op. cit., p. 6.

12. Ibid.

13. Ibid.

14. Massachusetts Institute of Technology Urban Systems Laboratory, USL-TR-71-03, op. cit., p. 610.

15. Merrick, Town of Hempstead, op. cit., p. 36.

16. Ibid., p. 35.

17. U.S. Congress, *Hearings on S.676*, op. cit., p. 89.

18. Ibid., p. 95.

19. This finding may be contrasted with a 1963 survey figure of only 9 percent choice riders among all transit users in the Milwaukee urbanized area. Southeastern Wisconsin Regional Planning Commission origin-destination surveys, as reported in Housing and Urban Affairs Committee Hearings, op. cit., p. 95.

20. Ibid., pp. 98, 99.

21. Housing and Urban Affairs Committee Hearings, op. cit., p. 96.

22. Ibid., p. 94.

23. Ibid., p. 102.

24. Bureau of Traffic Engineering and Electrical Services, City of Milwaukee, March 1969, as cited in Housing and Urban Affairs Committee Hearings, op. cit., p. 115.

25. Metropolitan Transit Authority of Maryland, *The Metro Flyer*, P.A.

26. Metropolitan Washington Council of Governments, *The Capital Flyer Bus Service*, prepared for the Urban Mass Transportation Administration (Project No. DOT-UT-59), November 1971, p. 54.

27. Appropriation Hearings, H.R. 9667, p. 1093. (Only 30 percent were five years old or less.)

28. U.S. Department of Transportation, UMTA, Approval Memo: Capital Grant Project SC-UTG-1, Dated June 4, 1970. Some ridership figures were as follows: 1960–204,753; 1962–204,690; 1967–206,830.

29. U.S. Department of Transportation, UMTA Approval Memo Dated January 6, 1972, Capital Grant Project CAL-UTG-42.

30. Progress Report of the Greater Wilmington Transportation Authority, January 26, 1971, p. 2.

31. American Society of Medical Technologists, *Cadence*, September-October, 1970, p. 22.

32. District of Columbia, Preliminary Application for a Washington, D.C., Downtown Transit Capital Grant, Forwarded July 23, 1971.

33. Ibid., based on data by the Metropolitan Washington Council of Governments.

34. Ibid., p. 2c.

35. Ibid., p. 3c.

36. U.S. Department of Transportation, UMTA, Approval Memo for Capital Project PR-UTG-9, Dated August 25, 1971.

37. W.C. Gilman & Co., "Improvements to Public Transportation in the San Juan Metropolitan Area" (draft), May 1971.

38. U.S. Department of Transportation, UMTA, Approval Memo for Capital Grant Project RI-UTG-2, Dated December 17, 1969.

39. U.S. Congress, House Subcommittee of the Committee on Appropriations, 91st Congress, 1st Session, 1971, Part III, p. 211.

40. Alan M. Voorhees, op. cit.

41. U.S. Congress, House Subcommittee of the Committee on Appropriations, 91st Congress, op. cit., Part III, p. 211.

42. U.S. Department of Transportation, UMTA, Approval Memo on Capital Grant Project CAL-UTG-25 dated July 16, 1970.

43. San Diego Transit Corporation Annual Report for the Fiscal Year ending June 30, 1968.

Chapter 6
Commuter Rail

1. "Skokie Swift to Continue," *American City* 81, 6 (June 1966): 54.

2. "Skokie Gets Them Coming and Going," *Railway Age* 165, 14 (October 7, 1968): 34.

3. In Philadelphia, 85 percent of all commuter and transit cars were over 25 years old in 1960. American Municipal Association, "The Collapse of Commuter Service," Washington, D.C., 1960.

4. Frank Weir, "Rail Commuting: A Downward Trend Reversed," *Going Places* (General Electric Company), Third Quarter, 1962, pp. 10-11.

5. Fred Houser, "PATCO Plans Its Next Phase," *Railway Age*, February 8, 1971.

6. Louis T. Klander, "The Lindenwold Line, Successful Rapid Transit," *Traffic Quarterly*, Third Quarter, 1971, p. 332.

7. Ibid., pp. 334-36.

Glossary

ACI	Automatic car identification system
ADL	Arthur D. Little
ATA	American Transit Association
ATC	Automatic train control
ATO	Automatic train operation
ATP	Automatic train protection system
ATS	Automatic train supervision system
BART	Bay Area Rapid Transit, San Francisco
BARTD	Bay Area Rapid Transit District
CBD	Central business district
CEA	Central employment area
cps	Cycles per second
CTA	Chicago Transit Authority
CTS	Cleveland Transit System
dba	A-scale weighted decibels for measuring noise levels
dbc	C-scale weighted decibels for measuring noise levels
DRA	Development Research Associates
DRPA	Delaware River Port Authority
DTS	Data transmission system
EPA	U.S. Environmental Protection Agency
Hz	Octave band measure; the audible band is divided into eight bands from 20 to 10,000 Hertz; used in computation of annoyance and loudness levels
IRT	Institute for Rapid Transit
JET	Job Express Transportation demonstration project, initiated in Baltimore in 1970
MARTA	Metropolitan Atlanta Rapid Transit Authority
MBTA	Massachusetts Bay Transportation Authority
mphps	Rate of acceleration expressed in miles per hour per second
MTA	Mass Transit Authority (Baltimore, New York, etc.)
ppm	Parts per million; used for measuring air pollution
ROW	Right-of-way
SEPTA	Southeastern Pennsylvania Transportation Authority
SMSA	Standard Metropolitan Statistical Area, designating the urban area with a population over 250,000
SRI	Stanford Research Institute
UMTA	Urban Mass Transit Administration; U.S. Department of the Transportation
WMATA	Washington Metropolitan Area Transit Authority

147

Bibliography

Abt Associates. *Travel Barriers: Transportation Needs of the Handicapped.* Cambridge, Massachusetts, August 1969.

Adkins, W.G. et al. *Value of Time Savings of Commercial Vehicles.* Washington, D.C.: Highway Research Board, Report No. 33, 1967.

"Aerospace Crowds Into Mass Transit." *Business Week*, September 18, 1971, pp. 20-21.

"Aerospace Turns to the Ground." *Engineering News-Record*, May 13, 1971, p. 13.

"Air Cushion Vehicle Test Track Inches Forward." *Engineering News-Record*, December 16, 1971, p. 28.

Allegheny County, Port Authority. *South Hills Transit Expressway Revenue Line.* Volume I, January 1970.

American Municipal Association. "The Collapse of Commuter Service." Washington, D.C., 1960.

American Society of Medical Technologists. *Cadence.* September-October 1970.

American Transit Association. *Transit Fact Book* (Annual). New York City.

"Around the World . . . Sic Transit Rapid Transit." *Engineering News-Record*, April 7, 1960, p. 26.

Arrow, Kenneth J. "Criteria for Social Investment." *Water Resources Research*, First Quarter, 1965.

Arthur D. Little, Inc. *Center City Transportation Studies* Volume I. Cambridge, 1970.

"Artist's Conception of a Typical Washington Area Metro Station." *Construction*, July 17, 1968, p. 52.

Asher, Joe. "If Transit Comes, Can A Real Estate Developer Be Far Behind?" *Railway Age*, November 8, 1971.

Ashford, Norman and Frank M. Holloway. "The Effect of Age on Urban Travel Behavior." *Traffic Engineering*, April 1971, pp. 46-67.

Aten, Beach W. et al., *WMA Transit Company.* Washington, D.C.: Consortium of Universities, August 1970.

Atlanta, Metropolitan Rapid Transit Authority. *The Atlanta Plan: Rapid Transit for the People.* July 1970.

"Automatic Train Operation Can Help Find Economic Solutions to Growing Urban Mass Rail Transit Problems." *Metropolitan*, November-December, 1969, pp. 19-20.

Automobile Manufacturers Association. *1967 Automobile Facts and Figures.* Detroit, 1967.

Baker, Charles D. "Remarks before the Fifth Management Conference of Financial Prospects for Transportation, Northwestern University, Evanston, Illinois, March 16, 1970." *High Speed Ground Transportation Journal*, May 1970, pp. 314-25.

Baker, Robert F. et al. "Transportation Research Needs in Civil Engineering." *Transportation Engineering Journal of ASCE* 97, TE3 (August 1971): 541-72.

Baltimore, Maryland, Department of Transit and Transportation. *Job Express Transportation* (Final Report). June 1971.

Barr, William. *Parking: Public vs. Private.* Cited in "A Look at Urban Transportation," by Ardie Ames. Reprinted from *Nation's Cities*, July 1, 1965, p. 14.

"BART: The Prototype Route Pays Off." *Railway Age*, May 10, 1971.

"BART: Catalyst for Bay Area Planning." *Rapid Transit*, 1968.

Barton-Aschman Associates, Inc. *The Impact of Transportation Staging on Metropolitan Growth.* Prepared for the Metropolitan Area Planning Council, Boston, Massachusetts, February 1970.

Barton-Aschman Associates, Inc. *A Transit Improvement Program for the Tulsa Metropolitan Area*, 1970-1974. Chicago, Illinois, October 1970.

Baum, Milton S., Albert Gutowsky, and Gerald Rucker. *Cost and Benefit Evaluation of the Sacramento Transit Authority.* Interim Technical Report #4, Sacramento State College, October 1970.

"Bay Area Rapid Transit." *Modern Railroads*, January 1972.

Bay Area Rapid Transit District. "BART and the Ghettos." *Rapid Transit* (An Information Digest from BARTD). Special Issue, Summer, 1969, Volume II, No. 3.

"A Big Drop in Public Transit Use." *American City*, October 1965.

"Boston: A Master Plan Puts Spokes into the Hub." *Railway Age,* June 6, 1966, p. 20.

"Boston Converts Commuter Lines to Rapid Transit." *Railway Age*, October 11, 1971, pp. 18-20.

"Boston Mounts a $340-Million Attack on Transportation Confusion." *Engineering News-Record*, September 1, 1966, pp. 32-34.

Boston Redevelopment Authority. *The Feasibility of Moving Sidewalks on the South Station-Summer Street Area of Downtown, Boston.* January 1971.

Boston Urban Foundation Study. *Center City*. 1969.

California, State of, Business and Transportation Agency. *Transportation-Employment Project: South Central and East Los Angeles.* Prepared for Urban Mass Transportation Administration, August 1971.

Carnegie-Mellon University, Transportation Research Institute. *Latent Demand for Urban Transportation.* Pittsburgh, May 1968.

Charles River Associates, Inc. *Prospects for Urban Transit.* Cambridge, Massachusetts, 1970.

Chicago Transit Authority. *Chicago Central Area Transit Planning Study.* Volume II, Chicago, 1970.

Chicago Transit Authority. *Skokie Swift "The Commuter's Friend."* Chicago, May 1968.

City Planning Department of Oakland. *People, Jobs, and Transportation: An*

Examination of Transportation as a Factor in Oakland's Unemployment.
December 1969.

Clark, Coleman & Rupeiks, Inc. *Transit Study for Billings, Montana.* Seattle,
January 1969.

Cleveland Transit System. *Southwest Rapid Transit Extension: Feasibility
Report.* December 1960.

Columbus, Georgia. *Columbus Youth Opportunity 1970.* Information Package.

"Commuters (20,000) Vote for Rail Transit." *Railway Age*, April 7, 1969, pp.
24-25.

Cooper, Ernest, Jr. *Methods of Improving Transportation Facilities for Inner-
City Dwellers.* Washington, D.C.: Consortium of Universities, August 1970.

Cuyahoga County Regional Planning Commission. *Cleveland Hopkins Airport
Access Study.* Survey results prepared for U.S. Department of Transportation, June 1970.

Davis, Frederick W. "Proximity to a Rapid Transit Station as a Factor in
Residential Property Values." *Appraisal Journal*, October 1970, pp. 554-72.

Day & Zimmermann Consulting Services. *Report to the City of Wilmington and
New Castle County, Delaware, on the Transit Situation in the City of
Wilmington and New Castle County.* Philadelphia, Pennsylvania, November
1967.

DeLeuw, Cather & Company. *Cleveland Transit System: Feasibility Study,
Euclid Avenue Extension and the Downtown Distribution Loop.* 1959.

DeLeuw, Cather & Company. *Long-Range Transportation Plan for the Central
Business District Dallas, Texas.* Prepared for the City of Dallas. Chicago, July
1965.

DeLeuw, Cather & Company. *Report to the Old Colony Area Transportation
Commission on Plans for Improved Suburban Transit.* April 1959.

DeSalvo, Joseph S. *Proceedings of a Conference on Regional Transportation
Planning—January 25-27, 1971.* Santa Monica, California: Rand Corporation,
May 1971.

Development Research Associates. *Benefits to the Federal Government from the
Adopted Regional Metro System* (Technical Appendix). Prepared for
Washington Metropolitan Area Transit Authority. Washington, D.C., October
1968.

District of Columbia. *Preliminary Application for a Washington, D.C., Downtown Transit Capital Grant.* Forwarded July 23, 1971.

Dodson, E.N. "Cost-Benefit Sales for Urban Transportation." *Systems Analysis
of Urban Transportation.* Prepared for HUD. Volume 3. California: General
Research Corp., January 1968, pp. 103-139.

Douglas, Walter S. "Public Transportation as Part of Total Urban Transportation." *Traffic Quarterly*, October 1971, pp. 551-61.

EBASCO Services, Inc. *Rapid Transit System Economic Review: San Francisco
Bay Area Rapid Transit District.* June 1961.

EBASCO Services, Inc. *San Francisco Bay Area Rapid Transit District: Rapid Transit System Economic Review.* June 1961.

"Economic Effect of Rapid Transit on Real Estate Development." *Appraisal Journal*, April 1968, pp. 212-24.

"Extension of D.C. Rapid Transit Planned." *Civil Engineering*, February 1968, pp. 90-91.

Floyd. "Using Transportation to Alleviate Poverty: A Progress Report on Experiments Under Urban Mass Transportation Act." *Transportation and Poverty Conference*, June 7, 1968.

"The Future of Urban Transportation." *Public Interest*, Winter 1970, pp. 52-87.

General Electric Company, Transportation Systems Division. *A Study of and Control Systems for Urban Transportation.* February 1968 (Project II: Express Bus Priority). Prepared for the U.S. Dept. of Housing and Urban Development.

General Electric Company. "Will People Forsake Their Automobiles for Good Rail Transit." *Going Places*, 4th Quarter, 1969, pp. 21-22.

Gibbs & Hill, Inc. *Conceptual Design of Automatic Train Control and Communications Systems*, New York, June, 1969.

Gibbs & Hill, Inc. *Feasibility of an Automated Yard Information and Control System (YICS).* Washington Metropolitan Area Transit Authority. New York, 1969.

Gilman, W.C. & Company. *Denver Transit Study.* Denver, 1970.

Gilman, W.C. & Company. "Improvements to Public Transportation in the San Juan Metropolitan Area." (Draft), May 1971.

Graham, Philip A. *Methodological and Parametric Foundations for Urban Technology Evaluation.* Washington, D.C.: Consortium of Universities, August 1970.

Hamburg, John R., Geoffrey Brow, and Morton Schneider. "Impact of Transportation Facilities on Land Development." *Highway Research Record*, No. 305, 1970, pp. 172-78.

Hammond, David G. "BART Demonstration Programs." *Transportation Engineering Journal of ASCE* 97, TE4 (November 1971): 627-50.

Haney, Dan G. "Problems, Misconceptions and Errors in Benefit-Cost Analyses of Transit Systems." *Highway Research Record*, No. 314, 1970, pp. 98-113.

Hartgen, David T. and George H. Tanner. "Individual Attitudes and Family Activities: A Behavioral Model of Traveler Mode Choice." *High Speed Ground Transportation Journal*, September 1970, pp. 439-67.

Harvey, Thomas N. *Estimation of User Benefits From Alternative Urban Transportation Systems.* Final Report Prepared for Network Evaluation Branch, Urban Planning Division, Federal Highway Administration. Philadelphia: Drexel University, April 1971.

Hauser, Edwin W., Leonard B. West, Jr., and A. Richard Schleicher. "Fundamental Air Pollution Considerations for Urban and Transportation Planners." *Traffic Quarterly*, January 1972, pp. 71-84.

Heenan, G. Warren. "The Economic Effect of Rapid Transit on Real Estate Development." *The Appraisal Journal*, April 1968.

Heenan, G. Warren. "The Impact of Transit: Real Estate Values." *Transportation: Lifeline of an Urban Society*. Pittsburgh Urban Transit Council, Fourth International Conference on Urban Transportation, Official Proceedings, 1969, pp. 129-34.

Herr and Fleisher. "The Mobility of the Poor." Paper presented at the Transportation and Poverty Conference of the American Academy of Arts and Science, June 7, 1968.

Hill, Morris. "A Method for the Evaluation of Transportation Plans." *Highway Research Record*, Number 180, 1967, pp. 21-34.

Hill, Terrell W. "The Impact of Transit: The Central Business District." *Transportation: Lifeline of an Urban Society*. Pittsburgh Urban Transit Council, Fourth International Conference on Urban Transportation, Official Proceedings, 1969, pp. 140-46.

Houser, Fred. "PATCO Plans Its Next Phase." *Railway Age*, February 8, 1971.

"Innovative Transit Planning Attracts Riders." *Passenger Transport*, January 21, 1972.

Institute for Rapid Transit. "The Economic Justification of Rapid Transit." *Proceedings of the Second Annual Conference*. Washington, D.C., May 10, 1963.

Kamrass, M., J. Crane, P. Hughes, and E. Parker. *Concepts for Evaluating Center City Transportation Programs and Projects* (Interim Report). Virginia: Institute for Defense Analysis, Urban Mass Transportation Project, December 1969.

Klauder, Louis T. "The Lindenwold Line Successful Rapid Transit." *Traffic Quarterly*, 3rd Quarter, 1971.

Kansas City Region, Metropolitan Planning Commission, Kansas City Area Transportation Authority. *Transit Improvement Plan, Metroplan 1971*. February 1971.

Krambles, George. "Transit Marketing in Chicago." *Transportation Engineering Journal of ASCE* 97, TE2 (May 1971): 361-70.

LaPlante, John N. "Exclusive Bus Lanes," Highway Research Board, *Improved Street Utilization Through Traffic Engineering*, Special Report #93. Washington, D.C., 1967, pp. 75-83.

Law, Edward M. "Real Estate and Population Growth Along Rapid Transit Lines in the City of New York." *The Municipal Engineers Journal*, Volume 21.

Liberty Mutual Insurance Company Newsletter, 1st Quarter, 1972.

Lindsay, Robert. "Easy Ride On A Philadelphia Transit Line." *New York Times*, February 16, 1970.

Lisco, T.E. *The Value of Commuters' Travel Time, A Study in Urban Transportation*. Ph.D. dissertation, University of Chicago, June 1967.

MacDonald, Scott. "Urban Mass Transit: A Multi-billion Dollar Investment." *Government Executive*, June 1971, pp. 31-33.

McKean, Roland N. *Efficiency in Government Through Systems Analysis.* New York: John Wiley, 1958.

Madigan-Hyland, Inc. *A Study of Metropolitan New York Transportation.* Prepared for Triborough Bridge and Tunnel Authority, March 1967.

Mantell, Edmund H. "Economic Biases in Urban Transportation Planning and Implementation." *Traffic Quarterly,* January 1971, pp. 117-30.

Maryland Metropolitan Transit Authority. "The Metro Flyer: A Suburban Express Bus Service to Downtown." Project No. MD-MTD-1, Project period May 1966-April 1967.

Mason, Ralph and William B. Stewart. "Computer Simulation of Transit Operations and Costs." *American Society of Civil Engineers Journal,* Proceedings, February 1969, pp. 57-66.

"Mass Transportation Report." *Product Engineering,* December 1971, p. 18.

Massachusetts, State of, Joint Special Committee on Transportation. *Summary of the Report on Transportation to the General Court on the Organizational and Financial Structure of the M.T.A.* January 1962.

Massachusetts Bay Transportation Authority. *Determination of Optimum Performance Criteria: Proposed Orange Line Transit Cars.* February 1968.

Massachusetts Institute of Technology Urban Systems Laboratory, USL-TR-70-18. *Implications of Dial-A-Ride for the Poor.* Cambridge, Massachusetts, March 1971.

Massachusetts Institute of Technology Urban Systems Laboratory, USL-TR-71-03. *Dial-A-Ride: An Overview of a New Demand-Responsive Transportation System.* Cambridge, Massachusetts, March 1971.

Merrick, Town of Hempstead, Nassau County, New York. *The Merrick Minibus: A Small Feeder Bus Operation for Commuters* (Final Report of Mass Transportation Demonstration Project NY-MTD-11). New York, May 1971.

Metropolitan Atlanta Rapid Transit Authority. *The Atlanta Plan—Rapid Transit for the People.* July 1970.

Metropolitan Transit Authority of Maryland. *The Metro Flyer.*

Metropolitan Washington Council of Governors. *The Capital Flyer Bus Service.* Prepared for the Urban Mass Transportation Administration, November 1971.

Michigan Southeastern Transportation Authority. *Application for a Mass Transportation Capital Improvement Grant.* July 1971.

"A Modern Rapid Transit Car and Its Automatic Control System." *Western Construction,* September 1965, p. 128.

"Move People Efficiently in Our Center Cities." *American City.* November 1970, p. 69.

Muehlberger, Ron. "MBTA, Public Transit Access to Airports." Highway Research Board, 1969.

National Analysts, Inc. *The Needs and Desires of Travelers in the Northeast Corridor: A Survey of Dynamics of Mode Choice Decisions.* Prepared for the Office of High Speed Ground Transportation, Federal Railroad Administration, Philadelphia, Pennsylvania, February 1970.

National League of Cities. "Center City Transportation." *Nation's Cities Magazine*, February 1970.

"National Survey on Exact Bus Fare System Shows Sharp Crime Reductions." *Police*, December 1971, p. 12.

The National Urban Coalition. *21 Cities: A National Perspective on Center City Transportation.* Washington, D.C., September 1970.

"New Cars Cut Costs for Boston." *Railway Age*, March 4, 1963, p. 16.

"A New Push for Public Transportation." *Business Week*, May 15, 1971, p. 74.

"A New Transit for Washington, D.C." *Railway Age*, January 4/11, 1965, p. 18.

New York City Transit Authority. *Annual Report 1966-1967.*

New York Metropolitan Commuter Transportation Authority. *Metropolitan Transportation: A Program for Action.* Report to Nelson A. Rockefeller, Governor of New York, February 1968.

New York Metropolitan Transportation Authority. *Annual Report 1967.*

New York Metropolitan Transportation Authority. *2 Years: Transportation Progress* (March 1968 to March 1970). March 1970.

Nixon, Richard. "Special Revenue Sharing for Transportation." (The President's Message to Congress, March 18, 1971). *Federal Register*, March 22, 1971, pp. 498-502.

Oakland, California, City Planning Department, Transportation Division. *People, Jobs, and Transportation: An Examination of Transportation as a Factor in Oakland's Unemployment.* December 1969.

Parsons, Brinckerhoff, Tudor, Bechtel. *San Francisco Bay Area Rapid Transit District Demonstration Project.* Technical report No. 12, final report, summary, January 1970.

Parsons, Brinckerhoff, Tudor, Bechtel, Sverdrup & Parcel. *St. Louis Metropolitan Area: Rapid Transit Feasibility Study, Long-Range Program*, PB204-060. St. Louis, August 1971.

Passenger Transport. The Weekly Newspaper of the Transit Industry, published by the American Transit Association, various issues.

"PATCO Plans Its Next Phase." *Railway Age*, February 8, 1971, pp. 17-19.

"People Mover System Heads for Construction." *Engineering News-Record*, August 26, 1971, p. 13.

Peat, Marwick, Livingston & Co. *Evaluation of a Bus Transit System in a Selected Urban Area.* Prepared for the Bureau of Public Roads, June 1969.

"People Will Forsake Their Automobiles For Good Rail Transit." *Metropolitan*, November/December 1969, pp. 21-22.

Perazich, George and Leonard L. Fischman. "Methodology for Evaluating Costs and Benefits of Alternative Urban Transportation Systems." *Highway Research Record*, No. 148. Washington, D.C.: Highway Research Board, 1966.

Perrot, Francis C. "The Flyda Mini-Bus System." *Traffic Quarterly*, January 1971, pp. 87-101.

Peterson, W.M., Consulting Engineers. *An Urban Mass Transit Study for the City of Brownsville, Texas.* DOT Project No. TEX-T9-4, Texas, August 1971.

Philadelphia Model Cities Program. *Application for a Mass Transportation Capital Improvement Grant.* Submitted: March 30, 1970, Revised: November 25, 1970, PA-UTG-24.

Pignataro, Louis J. and Edmund J. Cantilli. "Transportation and the Aging." *Traffic Engineering*, July 1971, pp. 42-46.

Pittsburgh Regional Planning Association (Preliminary Report). Volume 7, "Transportation," *Westmoreland County Comprehensive Plan Study.*

Plotkin, H.M. and Associates. *A Study to Determine Improvements to the San Bernardino Municipal Transit System for Increasing Employment Opportunities to Residents of Depressed Areas.* San Bernardino, California, 1968. PB-183-158.

The Port of New York Authority. *A Plan for an Exclusive Bus Lane on Interstate Route 495 from the New Jersey Turnpike to the Lincoln Tunnel.* January 1967.

Prest, A.R. and R. Ruvey. "Cost Benefit Analysis—A Survey." *The Economic Journal*, December 1965.

"Problems of the City and Today's Transit." *Civil Engineering*, September 1968, pp. 29-34.

Progress Report of the Greater Wilmington Transportation Authority. January 26, 1971.

"Proposals to Aid Mass Transit Include Taxes, Tax Privileges and Direct Grants." *Weekly Bond Buyer*, June 8, 1970, p. 7.

"Public Transport in Five Great Metropolitan Areas—Part II." *American City*, July 1960.

"Rapid Transit, Special Report." *International Railway Journal*, April 1971, entire issue.

Rasmussen, David W. *Joint Development: An Economic Input.* Tallahassee, Florida: Florida State University, June 1970.

Real Estate Research Corporation. "The Overall Impact on the Initial Transit Improvement Program on the Chicago Central Area," March 1968. *Chicago Central Area Transit Planning Study*, Volume III, Section IV, April 1968.

Regional Economic Development Institute. *Transportation Requirements and Effects of New Communities.* Pittsburgh, May 1968.

Resource Management Corporation. *Theory and Implementation of Cost and Benefit Analysis of Transportation Systems: The NECTP.* Prepared for Northeast Corridor Transportation Project, Bethesda, Maryland, December 1969.

Roberts, Robert. "LIRR Lives Up to Claim—'Finest in Land.'" *Modern Railroads*, August 1971, pp. 34-41.

Roddin, Marc. *Project IS/Improved Scheduling.* Cambridge: Massachusetts Institute of Technology, May 1970.

San Diego Transit Corporation Annual Report for the Fiscal Year Ending June 30, 1968.

Schneider, Lewis M. "A Marketing Strategy for Transit Management." *Traffic Quarterly*, April 1968, pp. 283-94.

Sexton, Burton H. "Traffic Noise." *Traffic Quarterly*, July 1969, pp. 427-39.

Simpson and Curtin. *Public Transit Master Plan*. Prepared for the Metropolitan Dade County Planning Department for the Miami Urban Area Transportation Study, Philadelphia, Pennsylvania, January 1969.

"Skokie Gets Them Coming and Going." *Railway Age* 165, 14 (October 7, 1968).

"Skokie Swift to Continue." *American City* 81, 6 (June 1966).

Smerk, George M. "An Evaluation of Ten Years of Federal Policy in Urban Mass Transportation." *Transportation Journal*.

Smerk, George M. *Urban Transportation: The Federal Role*. Bloomington: Indiana University Press, 1965.

Smith, Calvin O. "What Have Transit Demonstrations Really Shown?" *Transportation Engineering Journal of ASCE* 97, TE2 (May 1971): pp. 325-31.

Smith, Wilbur & Associates. *Lancaster Mass Transit Study*. Prepared for City and County of Lancaster, Pennsylvania, December 1969.

Smith, Wilbur & Associates. *The Potential for Bus Rapid Transit*. Detroit: Automobile Manufacturers Association, February 1970.

Smith, Wilbur & Associates. *San Jose-Santa Clara County Bus Study*. Prepared for the City of San Jose and the County of Santa Clara, San Francisco, September 1969.

Smith, Wilbur & Associates. *Shuttle Bus Service, Hunters Point Avenue to Manhattan, Queens-Long Island Mass Transportation Demonstration Program* (February 1965 to July 1966). March 1968.

Smith, Wilbur & Associates. *Urban Transportation Concepts* (Cited in Arthur D. Little, Inc., Center City Transportation Project).

"Some Considerations of On-Going Rapid Transit Planning and Design." *Traffic Engineering*, August 1970, p. 14.

Sorenson, J.L. "Identification of Social Costs and Benefits in Urban Transportation." *Systems Analysis of Urban Transportation*, Vol. 3. California: General Research Corporation, January 1968.

"South Jersey Transit Has Car Designed for New Service." *Railway Age*, May 6, 1968, pp. 19-21.

Southeastern Pennsylvania Transportation Authority. *Commuter Railroad Service Improvements for a Metropolitan Area, SEPACT I*. October 30, 1965.

Stanford Research Institute. *Benefit/Cost Analysis of the Five-Corridor Rapid Transit System for Los Angeles*. Prepared for the Southern California Rapid Transit District, California, May 1968.

Stanford Research Institute and University of California. *Reduction of Robberies and Assaults of Bus Drivers* (Final Report). Prepared for Alameda-Contra Costa Transit District, Menlo Park, California, December 1970.

Stone and Youngberg. *A Summary of Engineering, Financial and Technical*

Reports Submitted to the San Francisco Bay Area Rapid Transit District. October 1961.

Sweek, John Edgar. *Evaluating the Central City Access Opportunity Provided By a Public Transportation System.* Seattle: Washington University, 1970.

"Taking the Worry Out of Being Close." *Technology Preview*, May 1971, p. 59.

Thomas, T.C. *The Value of Time for Passenger Cars: An Experimental Study of Commuters' Values.* California: Stanford Research Institute, May 1967.

"$3-Million Study Will Look for Ways to Improve Air in Subway Systems." *Engineering News-Record*, October 28, 1971, p. 23.

"Tiny Bus Spurs City Shopping." *Business Week*, September 12, 1964.

"Track Powered Linear Induction Motors as a Rapid Transit Drive." *Engineering Journal*, April 1970, pp. 26-32.

"Transit: Pittsburgh Splits Over Skybus." *Business Week*, August 7, 1971, p. 25.

"Transportation." *Constructor*, September 1968, p. 17.

"Transportation Debt Holders Should Heed Closely the New Haven and Chicago Transit Developments." *Weekly Bond Buyer*, June 15, 1970, p. 16.

Tri-State Transportation Commission. *Coordinated Bus-Rail Service: Rockland County-Westchester County-New York City.* Final report on the Mass Transportation Demonstration Project (September 17, 1963-June 25, 1965). January 1967.

Tri-State Transportation Commission. *Park 'N' Ride Rail Service: Jersey Avenue Station, New Brunswick, New Jersey.* Final report on the Mass Transportation Demonstration Grant Project (October 27, 1963-April 24, 1965). May 1967.

Tri-State Transportation Commission. *People-Transportation-Jobs: Public Transport Services to Non-CBD Employment Concentrations.* A Mass Transportation Demonstration Grant Project, Nassau and Suffolk Counties Progress Report No. 4, October 1969.

Tri-State Transportation Commission. *Suburban Service Adjustment Experiment.* A final Report on the Mass Transportation Demonstration Grant Project. New York, November 1967.

Twin Cities Area Metropolitan Transit Commission. *Annual Reports* 1968, 1969, 1970, St. Paul, Minnesota.

Urban Mass Transportation Administration. "Research, Development and Demonstration Program." *Department of Transportation News*, July 1970.

"Urban Transport We Could Really Use." *Technology Review*, June 1970, p. 30.

U.S. Congress, House Committee on Appropriations. *Hearings on Department of Transportation and Related Agencies Appropriations.* 92d Congress, 1st Session, on H.R. 9667, Washington: GPO, 1971.

U.S. Congress, House Committee on Appropriations. *Hearings on H.R. 17755.* 91st Congress, 2d Session. Washington: GPO, 1970.

U.S. Congress, House Subcommittee of the Committee on Appropriations. *Hearings on Department of Transportation and Related Agencies Appropri-*

ations for 1972. 92d Congress, 1st Session. Washington, D.C.: GPO 1971.

U.S. Congress, House Subcommittee on Housing of the Committee on Banking and Currency. *Hearings on H.R. 6663, S. 3154, H.R. 7006, H.R. 13463, H.R. 16261.* Washington, D.C.: GPO, March 1970.

U.S. Congress, Senate Subcommittee on Housing and Urban Affairs of the Committee on Banking and Currency. *Hearings on S. 676, S. 1032, S. 2656, S. 2821, S. 3154.* 91st Congress, 1st Session. Washington, D.C.: GPO, 1969.

U.S. Department of Transportation. *Capital Grant Project Memoranda.* Various issues and dates.

U.S. Department of Transportation, Assistant Secretary for Environment and Urban Systems. *Broad and Columbia Subway Development Study: Philadelphia.* August 1971.

U.S. Department of Transportation, Assistant Secretary of Policy and International Affairs, Office of Systems Analysis and Information, Strategic Planning Division. *Recommendations for Northeast Corridor Transportation.* Summary Report, Volume 1, Washington, D.C., May 1971.

Vedder, James. "Planning Problems with Multidimensional Consequences." *Journal of the American Institute of Planners,* March 1970.

Villarreal, Carlos C., Urban Mass Transportation Administration. "The UMTA Bus Program." *Department of Transportation News.*

Voorhees, Alan M. "The Changing Role of Transportation in Urban Development." *Traffic Quarterly,* 23, October, 1969.

Voorhees, Alan M. & Associates, Inc. *Eugene-Springfield Transit Study Report.* Prepared for the Central Lane Planning Council. McLean, Virginia, December 1969.

Voorhees, Alan M. & Associates, Inc. *Feasibility and Evaluation Study of Reserved Freeway Lanes for Buses and Car Pools: Summary Report.* Prepared for U.S. Department of Transportation. January 1971.

Voorhees, Alan M. & Associates, Inc. *An Integrated Island Wide Bus System.* Prepared for the City and County of Honolulu, Hawaii. Honolulu, April 1971.

Voorhees, Alan M. & Associates, Inc. *A Transit Improvement Program for the Utah Transit Authority.* McLean, Virginia, March 1971.

Walker, Samuel A. *Crosstown Transit Study: Final Report on the 1965 Demand.* Chicago Area Transportation Study, Chicago, 1970.

"Washington Metropolitan Area Transit Authority." *Constructor,* September 1968, pp. 41-43.

"Washington Rapid Transit a Juicy Electronics Plum." *Electronic News,* August 19, 1968, p. 16.

Weir, Frank. "Rail Commuting: A Downward Trend Reversed." *Going Places* (General Electric Company), 3d Quarter, 1962, pp. 10-11.

Westinghouse Electric Corporation, Transportation Systems, *Report on Com-*

puter Simulation Studies of the Long Island Railroad. Prepared for Queens-Long Island Mass Transportation Demonstration Program, Pittsburgh, Pennsylvania, November 1966.

Wickstrom, George B. "Defining Balanced Transportation—A Question of Opportunity." *Traffic Quarterly*, July 1971, pp. 337-49.

Wiggers, George F. "Cleveland Rail Transit Airport Service." *U.S. Department of Transportation, Highway Research Board*, No. 330, 1970.

Wohl, Martin. "Current Mass-Transit Proposals: Answer to Our Commuter Problem?" *Civil Engineering—ASCE*, December 1971, pp. 68-70.

Young, Robert N. et al. "Evaluating Transportation Systems." *Transportation Engineering Journal of ASCE* 97, TE2 (May 1971): 347-52.

Young, Whitney, Jr. "Transportation: Making Cities Work for People." *Transportation: Lifeline of an Urban Society*. Pittsburgh Urban Transit Council, Fourth International Conference on Urban Transportation, Official Proceedings, 1969, pp. 118-28.

Index

161

About the Authors

Nancy W. Sheldon, project director for this study, is a senior associate at Harbridge House, Inc. She received a bachelor's degree from Wellesley College and the master's degree in economic geography from Columbia University. A doctoral candidate at Columbia, she is currently writing her dissertation on policy decisions and spatial dynamics of siting transporation facilities. She was a Durant Scholar at Wellesley and has been elected a Fellow to the Faculty at Columbia.

Robert Brandwein, a Vice President of Harbridge House, Inc., received a bachelor's degree in economics from Cornell University, the master's degree in economics from Brooklyn College, and has completed course work toward a doctorate in economics at The American University.